THE
MIRACLE
IN THE
MIDDLE

THE
MIRACLE
IN THE
MIDDLE

FINDING GOD'S VOICE IN THE VOID

Charlotte Gambill

W Publishing Group

An Imprint of Thomas Nelson

Published in Nashville, Tennessee, by W Publishing Group, an imprint of Thomas Nelson.

Thomas Nelson titles may be purchased in bulk for educational, business, fund-raising, or sales promotional use. For information, please e-mail SpecialMarkets@ThomasNelson.com.

Library of Congress Control Number: 201593295

ISBN 9780849921988

Printed in the United States of America

15 16 17 18 19 RRD 6 5 4 3 2 1

CONTENTS

CHAPTER ONE · ARE WE THERE YET? 1

CHAPTER TWO · FOLLOW ME. 21

CHAPTER THREE · KEEP YOUR SHOES ON 39

CHAPTER FOUR · STRAINING AT THE OARS. 57

CHAPTER FIVE · THREE THINGS 73

CHAPTER SIX · DROP ANCHOR. 91

CHAPTER SEVEN · PIGGY IN THE MIDDLE. 109

CHAPTER EIGHT · RESPONSE TIME. 127

CHAPTER NINE · COMMUNAL CHANGE 147

CHAPTER TEN · AFTER THE GIANT 167

CHAPTER ELEVEN · MIRACLE IN THE MIDDLE. 187

ABOUT THE AUTHOR 207

ONE

ARE WE THERE YET?

"ARE WE THERE YET?!" IT WAS AN OVERLY DRAMATIC, AGITATED cry from the backseat of our rental vehicle as two bored and tired children decided they had had enough of being strapped like prisoners into their child seats. Earlier that day, assuming we were adequately prepared for the long day ahead, Steve and I had set off on a six-hour road trip to our vacation destination. We had packed snacks and games, and planned the bathroom stops—all to help make the journey successful and less stressful. Yet even with the world's best planning there are eventualities you don't plan for—scenarios that can range anywhere from exploding drink cartons to unexpected backseat wrestling matches.

We were no exception. What we thought would be a family bonding experience was fast becoming a scene from a disaster movie. What had previously pacified our little passengers now had little to no effect on them. They no longer cared to look at the pretty scenery passing by and did not want to play I Spy from the elevated vantage point their car seats provided them.

And while my husband's out-of-tune and ambitious rendition of every Disney song in his limited repertoire wore thin, and one by one the backup supplies packed to ensure road-trip sanity fell short, we also ran out of the snacks that had previously bought us precious moments of silence. But the kiss of death was when the electronic devices we had put so much faith in to occupy our captive audience were each drained of their power. At that point, I knew exactly how they felt. Drained, and with my fuses about to blow, we started to look for some kind of sign from the freeway. We needed the golden arches, or even a Cracker Barrel, to save us as our desperate passengers' rhythmic chant of "Are we there yet?" intensified. Why had we ever thought a road trip with two small—but very mighty—children was a good formula for a relaxing family vacation? We had no clue.

THE INNER CHILD

In the same way, every one of us travels through life with an inner child in the backseat—an impatient passenger that dwells within us as we travel our paths, pursuing the destinations we believe we've been called to discover. That inner child is all too often distracted by the seeming snail's pace of our personal progress, or becomes bored by the monotonous scenery en route. We are frustrated by the testing terrain before us and often feel ill equipped to face the demands the journey may require. And though we may start out with high expectations, excited by the undiscovered potential that awaits us, we get stuck attempting to navigate problems more often than we find ourselves attaining promises. We end up exerting a lot of energy on unforeseen obstacles rather than enjoying the new horizons we'd hoped for. Maybe on your journey your business is failing more than flourishing, or the relationship that held such potential has run into trouble. Maybe the road has become uncomfortable and caused you to feel isolated and alone. You may feel as if you have entered some kind of void—a place where your spiritual GPS seems to have become disconnected, and you find yourself looking for any encouragement you can find to stick with your planned destination.

If you are currently spending more time searching for an exit ramp than enjoying the journey, this book is for you. I want to reengage the disengaged, encourage the discouraged, cheer on the fainthearted—those no longer convinced the dream is worth the commitment it demands. We have all been there, and it may even be that is where you find yourself right now. If so, can I reassure you that you are not alone? In fact, there are usually more of us in this muddled middle than those who have reached their dream destinations. This is why I am dedicating this book to you, my fellow traveler, because I want to strengthen your weary spirit and breathe hope into your soul. The dysfunction you are facing does not have to derail you and the future you still want to believe in is not out of reach, so do not stop reading now.

TEMPER TANTRUM

That day in the backseat of our car, our two children expressed their discontent loud and clear. You, however, may not be the type of person who gives such an audible voice to your frustration, yet your internal struggle is no less real. Though your

Are we there yet? questioning of God may be silent to those around you, it rarely stops resonating inside you. It can become a repetitive echo in your soul. It can be evidenced by the change in your demeanor, as your enthusiasm for the journey lessens. Now your ebbing faith causes your once confident stride to be replaced by faltering footsteps.

WE ATTEMPT TO FORCE WHAT GOD HASN'T ENDORSED.

At this point, your own barrage of questions begins toward our Heavenly Father, as you seek assurance that this journey has an end destination in sight. It is often in this void that we think we need to hear God's voice the most, and yet it can seem that it is here that He speaks the least. Just as when we, as parents, choose to not always respond to our children's demands to stop the vehicle or pacify their boredom, God doesn't always answer us immediately.

If we leave this internal turmoil unaddressed, it can quickly intensify from a quiet complaint to a temper tantrum with God. At this point, without intervention, the impatient traveler is tempted to take matters into his or her own hands, often with disastrous results. We attempt to force what God hasn't endorsed or prematurely leave the route He has planned for us, thinking we will find a shortcut to a breakthrough by ourselves. (By the way, I have tried the shortcut and my advice is to not take it!)

CROSSROADS

I know what it is to lose your stride in certain seasons of life, when the road simply seems too long to endure. I have felt the frustration of the prolonged promise waiting to be fulfilled, and I have asked God many times *Are we there yet?* only to find no satisfactory answer to help me decide whether I should persevere or give in. The fact is we are all on a journey from where we are now to where we want to be. And in our eagerness to get there, we must remember that God never promised it would be easy. We weren't given a fast pass to jump the part of the process we like the least. The journey of any dream, plan, and destiny will be filled with many highs and lows; it will take you from mountaintop to valley. The scenery may go from breathtaking to boring, but when we trust God with the process, every stage can be useful and instructive.

On my own journey I have met many people who are at the crossroads between their dreams and their current realities. They are confused travelers, disoriented by the season they are in. I have seen weary pastors ready to walk away from their callings, tired of the testing and disillusioned by their progress. I have listened to business leaders share how their frustrations were causing them to derail plans for the future. I have seen others quit projects and downscale their expectations because the journey had brought such disappointment that it corroded confidence and deflated dreams. At these crossroads we have to contend with that inner child in the backseat, who is more inclined to quit than to persevere.

Every journey typically goes through three stages. For the purposes of this book, I will call them *the beginning, the middle,* and *the end.* The beginning and the end act as the two great bookends to the section we're referring to as the middle. This middle stage can be short or long, but I have found it is usually longer than we want it to be. Though it has moments when it is exhilarating, it is usually exhausting. The middle is also not very glamorous and, therefore, not something we choose to dwell on.

The middle is the *Are we there yet?* part of our journey, and I believe, one of the most underestimated stages of our growth. Throughout our time together I want to elevate the middle stage and to ask you to reconsider the power in this place that you may even be resenting. I truly believe that in the middle is where you really find out what is in the middle of you.

THE BEGINNING

But first let's consider the role of these bookends called *the beginning* and *the end*. Every new beginning comes with its own range of emotions propelling you forward with an energetic enthusiasm into new adventures—whether it is the realizing of a formative idea or seizing a fresh start relationally or vocationally. The beginning whispers endless possibilities, unknown adventures, and exciting opportunities. Our conversations at the start are typically filled with great expectancy, as we surround ourselves with faith-building company to help build our dreams and incubate their futures.

The beginning is about commitment and affirmation; it's the place we declare intent and pledge to the journey on which we are about to embark. It is heard in the vows spoken at the start of a marriage, as two become one. It can be witnessed in the planning and activity of newly expectant parents. It is written in the contract that provides the starting point for a business venture. Whether it is a new baby, relationship, church, or business, the beginning offers everyone the momentum that is uniquely found in a new start—the blank piece of paper that invites you to fill it with your creativity.

Beginnings give us the grace to say good-bye to the past and close previous chapters. They invite newly awakened curiosity to come and explore what lies ahead. Like a shot of adrenaline, they help activate and stimulate our faith. A strong start can even push dormant doubts into the background of our lives, which is often where they stay until our journey is well under way. Beginnings are where our hearts shout *Let's go!* as they wake up our potential and seize the awaiting opportunity.

NEW UNIFORM

As a mother, every September as my children prepare to go back to school, I am reminded of the joy and expectancy found in beginnings. The night before their school year begins they lay out their crisp uniforms with new school shoes and set their coats out at the front door. And even though they may be staying within the same school, they go to bed early with a nervous excitement as to what the morning will bring. The opportunity to begin again with a new teacher and class brings a fresh energy into their journeys. That next morning we take pictures of them leaving for the first day, and then we wait for them after school to hear all the news of how the day went.

Beginnings bring with them all these moments and more, which is why we must never underestimate the gift they give us and instead maximize every opportunity they afford us. Because in our home, it is not long before the same school uniform, which was previously ironed and hung carefully in the closet, is now thrown carelessly on the bedroom floor. And the new shoes are well-worn from the lunchtime soccer games they have been subjected to. The excitement for the new teacher is also wearing thin. Yes, it is true that beginnings don't last long, but for a moment in time they serve to propel us forward with high hopes and expectations. This gift of hope is what we as travelers must learn to harness, because it serves as something to hold onto when we reach the more challenging middle moments.

TURN IT UP

God turns up the volume at the start of a new journey, which is why it can be so exciting. It is here we can hear His voice loud and clear. We receive words of affirmation about the direction He is calling us and feel a sense of confirmation and witness from those around us. With the volume turned up, God's Word stirs up our faith, silencing the reasons why we shouldn't or couldn't do what we are intending

WHAT GOD GIVES US IN THE BEGINNING IS SOUL FOOD TO SUSTAIN US LATER.

to do. What God gives us in the beginning is soul food to sustain us later. Therefore beginnings are the times when we must remember to press Record: Record the voice of God, the words of encouragement, and the signs that got you heading down this road. Record the instructions that mobilized you, because there may come a point in the middle where you will need to replay those directions to help you move again. There will be times when you use the words you recorded, which hold with them your purpose, to soothe the pain you may have to endure in the process.

Have you ever been driving in your car, listening to the radio, and just as you are singing along to your favorite song the station you'd selected loses its signal? Instead static, that awful white noise, comes blaring through your car's speakers. Suddenly you go from happily singing along to the track being barely recognizable. Usually it's because you've come into an area with poor reception. And depending on how patient you are, you will choose one of several options—you will either keep driving, waiting for the radio signal to improve, or you will start twiddling with the dials to try to find a different station, settling for having to listen to a different song. Or maybe you will switch the radio off altogether. Now you can't choose your preferred station, because the static is restricting your choices. The middle is where static happens and where our once-clear commitments are now compromised by circumstances that try to confuse and drown out the choices we had made.

STATIC

Remember the garden of Eden, where Adam and Eve walked and talked with God daily? The signal between them and their Creator was loud and clear. Yet Satan came in the form of a serpent with one goal: create just enough static that Adam and Eve would sin, and in doing so, place a permanent defect in mankind's reception with God. Ever since then, the enemy has been intent on placing static into every spirit, because he wants you to lose the God signal for your life. If he can cause you to have poor reception through sin, doubts, compromise, or even weariness, he can derail you from your destiny. Adam and Eve knew what God had said about the Tree of Knowledge of Good and Evil, yet all it took was the static of a serpent's questioning to turn down the volume on God's plan and cause them to choose their own.

The enemy is the author of confusion. He is the source of the static and will wait for an opportune time to insert his interference—which is most often in the middle. After they ate of the fruit that day, Adam and Eve heard God's voice. Only when they heard Him this time, they hid and didn't dare to respond. The static had caused a separation that would go on to affect all of our destinations.

The enemy does not have any new tactics! They are still the same today. That is why in the middle we need to learn to stay tuned to the station where we last heard God speak to us. We need to leave the dial alone and reposition ourselves into a place of obedience that will allow us to regain reception. When I lose the signal in my car, I continue singing along to the song, even over the interference, and then wait to see if I have kept time with the original track when the signal becomes clear again. Often, I'm only a few words behind or ahead, but the point is I stuck to the song. How about if in our middles we do the same? We sing over the static; we keep speaking out what we know God spoke into our spirits. As we do, we will at some point be able to reconnect. I pray you will remember the song God gave you to sing, the instructions He told you to follow, and the things He has called you to do. As you read, I pray interference will be removed and the song of your future will be amplified.

THE END

The other bookend is much like beginnings in that it has its own energy. Endings offer us a place to stop and take it all in. They are where we can finally take our feet off the accelerators, relax our postures, and park for a while. Endings also bring satisfaction and a sense of achievement; they are the moments we capture in time that exclaim, "You did it! You made it happen!" They are where we realize that all of the work was not wasted and where we find a sense of reward for the roads we have traveled.

Happily ever after. This is the phrase every child and well-practiced storyteller knows is synonymous with great endings. So when we read fairy tales aloud to a captivated audience, even though the villains may seem to be gaining ground or harm looms over their favorite characters, the young listeners are comforted by the notion of what is to come. They draw hope from the way other fairy tales have ended and remind themselves that this is not the end. They persevere until closure arrives and sigh with great relief as all the loose ends are tied up and order is restored with those famous words, ". . . and they lived happily ever after." In reality, this is not always the closing statement at the end of our journeys. But for the most part, endings do bring a sense of satisfaction and a unique joy. They mark the arrival at a destination that has often been greatly anticipated.

Consider the ending for the pregnant woman; it is a moment that brings such a sense of relief and joy as she holds the long-awaited baby in her arms. She has finally come to the end of a journey that started with such excitement but quickly moved to exhaustion, from sleepless nights, a stretching waistline, cravings, and labor pains. Now at the end of the nine months, her energy seems to return as the moment she has dreamed of becomes reality. The moment where she sees and holds what she has carried for so long makes it all worthwhile.

Or what about the real relief and sense of achievement that an ending can bring for the nervous learner driver who finally gets the news he or she has been waiting for—the driving test has been passed? In that moment, all those long hours in driver's school, practicing for hours reverse and parallel parking, have finally paid off. As the certificate is signed and the license validated, the new driver is handed the freedom that makes all the bitter moments sweet.

I often go running and set myself a four-mile circuit. I set out with much enthusiasm, but typically in the middle my pace slows as I become more aware of how far I still have to go. I begin to lack the energy to keep up the pace. But by slowing down, I inevitably lengthen the very part of the process I want to make go faster. Yet without fail, when I realize I am almost to the end of my route, I find a renewed sense of enthusiasm and experience a surge of adrenaline. It's as though the sight of the finish line is enough to make my last mile more enjoyable and productive than all the miles in between.

Endings have that effect on us. When you see how close you are to completion, you ditch the drama and stop contemplating quitting (which was a very real option a few miles earlier). You also realize how foolish it was to drag your feet when the end was so much closer than you perceived it to be. I love endings. I love turning in the book I just finished writing, I love closing the deal, and I especially love throwing the parties that say, "You did it! You made it! You arrived!"

GRADUATE

The truth, though, is that not everybody gets to enjoy their ending moments. I remember when I was at university, so many students would arrive full of excitement, giddy at the prospect of their newfound freedom. In the beginning, they would busy themselves with settling into their new accommodations, finding out where the best places to hang out were, and embarking on their new social lives. It was always the same with every new batch of students. They all started with such high hopes, yet many would not make it to the graduation ceremony—never able to wear the cap and gown or receive the degree that was the original goal they set out to attain. The story of why they didn't make it was a tale all too familiar. Somehow in the middle, between their starts and finishes, they had lost the passion to proceed. They had become distracted, and their undisciplined choices meant they had lost sight of where they were supposed to be heading.

The middle years at university claimed many students, who would later be labeled dropouts. They were sent to the sidelines as their colleagues got to stand on the stage and graduate. What always sobered me was that those who quit somewhere in the middle did not get an exemption card from the costs that period incurred. They still had to pay a price for the process, but because they quit, they never got the prize.

Endings are prizewinning moments that justify the price you had to pay to get there. They are where the sweat and sacrifice you've invested become success. Without the endings, the cost of the middle makes no sense—just as with those students who were denied the party that perseverance would have thrown them. Where's the fun in that?!

PARTY PLANNER

Those who know me call me the party queen. I am not sure who gave me this regal title or when it was bestowed, but I will happily accept the label as I am a great believer in the power of a party. Whether it is a party to celebrate a friend's achievement, a party to thank people for all their hard work, or a party because it's been a while since the last party, it really doesn't matter! Our house is the party house. So one of the deciding factors if we ever were going to move would be whether there's a space somewhere big enough for our party needs. A typical party at our house would involve good food and lots of laughter. But, for me, the main point of the party is that every person feels celebrated, encouraged, and refreshed. I want them to take a moment to breathe and rejoice on the journey. That's why I believe endings should always come with a compulsory party!

Farmers celebrate the harvest being brought in, builders celebrate with a ribbon-cutting ceremony, students celebrate the academic graduation, and we as believers should throw parties as we reach milestones in our own journeys. Too often we forget to insert these full-stop moments as we are too preoccupied rolling into the next project or commitment. Yet without endings, our lives become exhausting, ultimately unsustainable, and a lot less fun.

THE MIDDLE

By now you will have a good notion of what this middle stage looks like. In the middle are the many and varied stories of adventure—lessons we'll learn and tales of trials we'll face. The bookends of beginnings and endings provide a sense of stability to these stories your middle will cause you to write. Though the pages of process in the middle are what we would most like to skip, without them our journeys would have no real content—comprised of the stories that would help anyone who might read from the pages of our lives.

Unlike the other stages, the middle doesn't offer the excitement of new beginnings or the joy found in endings. The middle is full of reality checkpoints where we realize the journey we had envisaged is unlike the journey we've actually experienced. I'm passionate about helping you better understand the middle of your journey—a place where many plateau and others turn back.

GRAND OLD DUKE OF YORK

As a child, I remember learning the nursery rhyme "The Grand Old Duke of York." For those of you who are not familiar with the rhyme, it goes as follows:

> *Oh, the grand old Duke of York*
> *He had ten thousand men*
> *He marched them up to the top of the hill*
> *And he marched them down again*
> *And when they were up, they were up*
> *And when they were down, they were down*
> *And when they were only halfway up*
> *They were neither up nor down*

This rhyme was clearly written by someone who was frustrated by the middle moments. It identifies the fact that in the middle you are neither one thing nor another. You lack definition and, therefore, direction. At least at the beginning and at the end the purpose is clear. But in the middle we can have many moments like the poor old Duke of York's men had.

The Grand Old Duke of York's men realized the middle is a place that is neither up nor down. We often have to face that same reality. We can reach the place where, for all our sowing, we seem to find there is no reaping. It's where we planted the seed but can see nothing appear above the soil, where we invested the energy but have yet to see any return for our work. It's the place that's neither a success nor a failure. If you have any control issues at all, as I do, this is one of the most annoying and exhausting parts about the middle—it does not allow us to tidy things up and will not give us the closure our controlling nature demands. Yet

I WANT MY MIDDLE TO BE A PLACE THAT BUILDS ME RATHER THAN BREAKS ME.

in those moments we have to let go of our need to be clear and allow our willingness to trust take over. And sometimes, as we want to make sense of things that are still developing, the labels we try to give in the middle cause more problems than they solve.

The middle can cause many to become muddled; it can be where confusion breeds and misunderstanding happens. The world has even tried to give the middle labels. If you are in the middle part of your life they invite you to have a midlife crisis—a label to cover any unfitting or unusual behavior that you may become susceptible to in this season. This badge can become a justification of the muddle we have created from our impatience and frustration. Yet I don't want my middle to be labeled a crisis; I want to find in the middle an ability to sustain my momentum. And I want my middle to be a place that builds me rather than breaks me. I have come to discover the amount of muddle in our middle is up to each of us—we can choose either a midlife crisis or a midlife success.

KEEP CLIMBING

I remember a few years ago being talked into climbing a mountain. I was excited to start the challenge, and I also felt a little competitive to try to climb faster than my friends who were accompanying me. At first, this adventure began with an enjoyable fast-paced walk along a meandering trail that was surrounded by breathtaking views. However, it soon became a much more testing adventure. It was when we were in the middle of our climb that I wanted desperately to go back down. I was no longer determined to make it to the top. I was tired of the loose rock we had to climb over and the places where instead of walking we were crawling on our hands and knees to make progress.

At this point we met a girl and her sister, who shared the same frustrations. To make matters worse, one of them had fallen and hurt her leg. She was literally on her bottom, moving one shuffle at a time, trying to come back down a steep ravine to ground level. We tried to point out that she was actually closer to the top than she realized, and if she went down in that manner she would hurt herself more. It was seeing her willingness to quit so close to the top that made me assess my own attitude and refocus my desire to make it to the end. As a group we tried to encourage our fellow climber. We even suggested that if she came with us, we could help her get to the top. After listening to and looking at our group (and maybe doubting our own ability to make it), she decided she didn't want to go any higher and that she was going back down to the base. So off she went, painstaking shuffle by shuffle, edging herself down the mountainside. All the energy she and her sister had exerted to get this far was about to be rendered worthless, as they would never get to where they had set out to go.

DO NOT BECOME SO WEARY AND DISILLUSIONED THAT YOU REFUSE THE HELP GOD WILL TRY TO SEND YOU.

Don't allow the middle to intimidate you; don't allow it to make you feel alone, and don't become so weary and disillusioned that you refuse the help God will try to send you. Just as we offered help to the injured climber to enable her to navigate to the top that day, God wants to extend His helping hand to every one of us. The journey may be hard, and in the middle we may face moments where we are brought to our knees, but those moments are just the pause in your story, not the ending.

MY PRAYER

My prayer is that you will take the hand of help within these pages and recognize you have come this far, so why not go for the finish? The view from the top awaits you, my friend. The enemy is a liar. In the middle is where he invites you to listen to his lies, telling you it's not worth it. But when I finally made it through the pain that was in the middle of the climb, I reached the top and the view was breathtaking. The view from your mountaintop is worth it, too, but if you want to see it you will have to learn to navigate your middle.

Navigating my middle moments is what has motivated me to sit and type these words to you. I am writing to every exhausted climber, weary traveler, and frustrated follower—the agitated and the aggravated ones. For those who are annoyed by their lack of progress and plagued by the disease called comparison. It is in the middle I have learned the most about myself, but also about my Master and Savior Jesus Christ. I want to extend an invitation to you to come with me for a while to explore the middle.

And as you read these words, I pray your spirit would be strengthened and your soul revived and that you would resolve to keep climbing, because the truth is with God no part of your journey (not even the most frustrating part) need ever be wasted. And I believe for those who are willing to embrace the adventure, you will soon discover there are miracles that await us all in the middle.

At the end of each chapter, you will find three points to consider putting into action and three points to pray over your journey. The Bible says that "faith without deeds is dead" (James 2:26). Therefore, as you read these pages, I encourage you to take the time to consider these action and prayer points as ways to help you further strengthen your own journey in the middle.

ACTION POINTS

1. Identify the middle you are currently facing.
2. Reduce the static in your life.
3. Commit to carry on climbing.

PRAYER POINTS

1. Pray for a new perspective for your middle.
2. Pray for clarity to hear God's voice.
3. Pray that the words within these pages will bring strength to your journey.

T W O

FOLLOW ME

IT WAS JUST AN ORDINARY DAY. THE YOUNG MEN WERE PRE-
paring their boats to go fishing. They cleaned their nets and loaded
their supplies onboard before pushing out from the shores of
Galilee. Only this day was not going to end in its usual manner
because their routine was about to be interrupted by a life-changing
invitation. Their predictable pace was going to be revolutionized
because of the power of two words: "Follow me" (Matthew 4:19).
These words that Jesus spoke offered the fishermen the opportunity of a new beginning—one which held within it the possibility
to change not only their lives but the lives of many others, including your life and mine. Those young men were going to become
part of the group of twelve men that Jesus would use to change the
course of history, and it all began with just two words.

"Follow me" was what Jesus said as He walked by the fishermen that day. It was the information they had to help them decide
if they were going to leave where they were for where He was heading. Jesus offered no further explanation of His expectations. But

on the basis of this brief encounter, the disciples would choose whether to leave family, friends, and their fishing business.

"Follow me" was asking for a shift of management; it was a step of faith to move from the familiar to the unfamiliar. Contrary to how it may have looked to those spectating that day, "Follow me" was not a random statement that Jesus casually threw out. Rather, these words were telling the disciples everything they would need to know about what this journey would require.

Jesus knew the type of characteristics His disciples would need. He knew what it would take to minister to crowds, navigate demands, and deal with the praise and the persecution. So when He walked by the fishermen's boat that day, the invitation was already written. The words were carefully selected—words that let them know the discipleship He was calling them into was a ministry not based on their qualifications or experience, but on their ability to follow.

As I have journeyed with Jesus over many years, I have come to realize that the place where our ability to follow is tested the most is often in the middle. The disciples would have to learn how to follow Jesus through highs and lows, through good and bad, and from start to finish. We as Jesus' disciples today also need to develop this same capacity to commit to improve our "follow" ability in every season we enter.

I HAVE DECIDED

I remember growing up in church singing the old hymn "I Have Decided to Follow Jesus." Maybe you remember the song? If not, the lyrics are pretty easy to understand.

I have decided to follow Jesus
I have decided to follow Jesus
I have decided to follow Jesus
No turning back, no turning back

I was in my kitchen at home awhile ago, tidying up after the children and clearing away some dishes, when that old tune came to mind and I started singing it to myself. As I got to the final chorus I started singing out loud: "Though none go with me, still I will follow, no turning back, no turning back." As I sang those lines, I felt God turn them around and nudge me with a question: *Charlotte, have you really decided no matter what that you will follow Me?*

My first response, if I'm honest, was to ignore the question as it did not seem appropriate or something I should be asked to answer. But as I felt God hold me on this thought I began to get a little offended, as the inference was that my following was somehow in question. *I mean, I am a pastor and leader; I work for the church; I write and speak all about Jesus; I mean, I am a Jesus girl!* But even though I tried to shake the question off, I couldn't help but feel that God wanted my attention on this issue. So after being offended for a little while longer, I decided to do something far more constructive: search my heart and seek God for what it was He wanted me to see.

It didn't take long before I discovered where the problem could possibly lie. It wasn't that I was away from God or deliberately rebelling in any area, but I began to see that in some areas, where I would *say* that I was following Jesus, the more truthful description would be that, actually, *I was expecting Jesus to follow me.*

WHO'S LEADING WHOM?

Have you ever traveled somewhere in a convoy, maybe on a road trip? Unsure of how to get to a certain destination, you ask a friend to take the lead. You agree the more confident navigator should be the first vehicle and everyone else will follow behind. I have had several experiences of traveling in a convoy and most have been unsuccessful. The journey begins well: the lead driver seems extra vigilant to keep the convoy together, aware of the others' lack of knowledge of the area—driving slow, not wanting to lose anyone. The leader waits at the turns and doesn't rush ahead at the lights. But after a while, when the journey takes you onto busier roads—moving from a one-lane road to several lanes of traffic—the whole "follow the leader" game changes.

Now with a sea of vehicles before you, following becomes a much more difficult task. Previously, you had paid as much attention to the conversation in your car as to the convoy you were supposed to be a part of. But now your distracted moments are becoming hugely detrimental to your progress. With increased speed and much more traffic, your lack of attention can mean losing the car you were following and missing your exit. Or even worse, as I have done before, you can end up following the wrong vehicle altogether!

I have found something similar can happen when it comes to following Jesus. We all remember those early seasons when we started our journeys of faith, when we first said yes to following Him. We leaned in to learn and we intentionally placed the vehicles of our lives behind His lead. We devoured His Word, sought His voice, and listened for His guidance. We were happy to give over the control of the steering wheels of our lives to His hands, as we were only too aware that we had caused enough wreckage while we were at the wheel.

Yet over time, as we become more skilled in our journeys, we can allow our confidence to turn to arrogance and replace our dependence on Jesus with misguided independence. We become prepared to widen the gap between His lead and our own leanings. We apply the same level of importance to His voice as we do to the opinions of others. We move from a focused faith to a more compromised place.

The more lanes we add to our lives—responsibility, relationships, friends, family, jobs, hobbies—the more ideas we launch and voices we listen to, and the more we can move from being disciplined followers to distracted followers. Becoming overfamiliar with the roads we are on, we begin to feel no need to check for the lead vehicle as regularly as we used to. Eventually we begin to accelerate in our own abilities, causing large amounts of time to be spent in lanes that God has already exited. If any of this sounds familiar, then maybe you, like me, would have to say there are times when you have lost track of Jesus.

LOSING JESUS

When Jesus was just twelve years old, He was following His parents on their annual pilgrimage to Jerusalem for the festival of the Passover. They had made this journey many times, and as was their custom, once the festivities were over, they would head back home. However, on this particular occasion, as Jesus' family went back to Nazareth, He did not join them. Rather, He stayed in the temple to listen to the words of wisdom spoken by the teachers and scribes. God was drawing Him, as a twelve-year-old boy, to have a greater desire for His Father's house than His Nazareth home.

When Jesus stayed behind in Jerusalem that day, no one realized He was missing. The Bible records that a whole day of traveling took place before anyone noticed that Jesus was not in the convoy headed back to Nazareth, and it was a full three days before they were able to find Him.

> After the festival was over, while his parents were returning home, the boy Jesus stayed behind in Jerusalem, but they were unaware of it. Thinking he was in their company, they traveled on for a day. Then they began looking for him among their relatives and friends. (Luke 2:43–44)

Imagine for a moment the sheer panic and shock when they finally realized they had lost Jesus! I picture the conversations that would have taken place between Mary and Joseph as one, no doubt, panicked and blamed the other for not keeping a closer eye on their boy. I can also envision the tense conversations as Mary asked, "Joseph, how could we lose the Savior of the World?!"

If Jesus' parents can lose Him, how much more can we make the same mistake? I know what you are thinking: *Jesus promised to be always with us.* And yes, that is true. Jesus will always have His hand on your life and mine. Hebrews 13 tells you that Jesus will never leave or forsake you (v. 5). But we can take our hands out of His. We can leave and forsake our faith; we can choose to wander away from where He wants to lead us. We can make decisions that move us away from His best plan for our lives and settle for our own preferred plan. It says in Galatians 5:25 to "keep in step with the Spirit," which suggests we can also be out of step with the Spirit. That is why following Him means we must learn how to keep putting our lives in the slipstream of His. Mary and Joseph did not keep their eyes on twelve-year-old Jesus. In the many distractions of the day, they lost sight of where He was, and rather than assure He was with them, they assumed He was with them.

ASSUMPTION

Assumption can be a deadly assassin to your destiny. We can all, over time, presume His presence. We presume He will bless our plans, work according to our schedules, keep our deadlines, and follow our lead when, in fact, it is our job to follow Him. Mary had lost Jesus that day simply because she had assumed He would be with her, only to discover that He had exited the path they were on much earlier. How many times can we be guilty of the same negligence? Where might the areas be that, even now, we are walking in assumption?

I am sure when Joseph and Mary assembled a search party, they went to look for Jesus in the places they presumed a twelve-year-old boy would be. Over the three-day search they probably checked the usual places—the local soccer fields and nearby watering holes where the other kids would be playing and swimming. Yet Jesus was not a typical twelve year old, and he was not in the usual places. He was not to be found where they deemed He should be; rather, He was found in the place His Heavenly Father had destined Him to be.

I have thought about this incident a lot when it comes to following Jesus in my own life. I have realized that at times I, like Mary, have presumed Jesus would be following me. I have assumed He would meet me in the usual ways I have seen Him move and speak before. I have expected Him to work on what I want to work on, and I have failed to stop and ask where He desires for me to labor. Even Mary, His own mother, would eventually have to accept that a shift was taking place. It was no longer time for Jesus, her boy, to follow her, but for her to follow Him—Jesus the Savior.

WAITING FOR YOU

One Christmas my husband, Steve, and I took our two children, Hope and Noah, to one of the largest shopping malls near where we lived for a day of treats and shopping. The mall was jam-packed with stressed-out shoppers; everyone was rushing around to complete their Christmas-list missions. We were in a clothing store with our children when my husband said he needed to go to the Apple store, which was about six stores farther down. I said, "I will meet you there." As he left, I saw my daughter go with him, so I assumed that my son was in tow as well. Ten minutes later I went to join them in the Apple store. Five minutes into our conversation I asked my husband, "Where's Noah?" His face told me everything I needed to know. When we had split up at the last store he had assumed I had Noah, while I had assumed

ASSUMPTION CAN BE A DEADLY ASSASSIN TO YOUR DESTINY.

he had Noah, and in that moment we realized neither of us had Noah!

At that time our son was six years old, and right in that moment panic struck my heart. I will never forget the incredible speed with which we both went from calm to freaked out. The mall was filled with people and there was a large gap between the two stores, providing multiple options for where he could have wandered. We set off back to the store where we had all last been together to find he wasn't there. We then checked every store in between, but still no Noah. I began to panic even more. I shouted his name, stopped every family passing by, and then after ten minutes (that felt like ten hours), I saw the small figure of a boy standing very calmly against a wall by the main intersection between the two stores we had been in.

I ran over and shouted "Noah!" and he calmly walked toward me. He didn't understand my tears and the many kisses I covered his face with. My husband hugged him, and then we asked him what had happened. He explained how he went to follow his dad but then lost him in the crowd, and so he then went to look for his mum but she had left the store. So he decided to wait in the middle of those two places until we came to where he was. He had full confidence that at some point we would all end up there, in the middle, so that's where he waited to be reunited.

This is so often how it is with God. While we want to rush ahead or even lag behind, we can lose track of the One we all along should have been following. The noise, the crowds, and the commotion of life can overwhelm us. Yet, the good news is Jesus is waiting right in the middle of it all for you to stop panicking and locate Him. In our relationship with God, when we lose track of Him, He doesn't panic or freak out. Instead, He waits for you to come and find Him; He waits for you to hear His voice and reconnect with His purpose and plan for your life.

HOME TIME

You remember the story of the prodigal son in Luke 15. The youngest son left home and drifted from one bad decision to the next. His journey took him farther and farther away from his father's house and from the place where he belonged. Yet as the son walks away from his family, you sense no panic in the father's heart. Though he longs for him to stay, he does not chase after him or go searching for him. The father understands that his son knows the address for home, and that is where the father chooses to wait for as long as it takes for his son to come back where he belongs.

The father waits with the reunion party already planned in his heart. He waits in love, and he waits in expectation that eventually there will come a moment when his son comes to his senses and heads home. When the prodigal finally returns, he is barely able to make it up the front pathway before an overjoyed father runs to embrace him. Jesus will often wait for you to come home and stop drifting off to places He never planned for you to end up. Just as our son, Noah, was in the middle waiting for us to find him, God is waiting for you. He won't judge or reprimand you; He will simply embrace you and invite you to follow Him once more. And this time, just like we did with Noah, you may find your grip on His hand is all the more tight, because in the middle you are reminded of why you never want to lose Jesus again.

POSTURE POWER

Our ability to follow well is either helped or hindered by our proximity to God. To ensure we are staying close to God, we need to keep adjusting our postures. We also have to keep checking our grips on His hand and deepen our ability to discern His voice to prevent familiarity from compromising the ability to follow. In Psalm 27 David writes:

> I'm asking GOD for one thing,
>   only one thing:
> To live with him in his house
>   my whole life long.
> I'll contemplate his beauty;
>   I'll study at his feet.
>
> That's the only quiet, secure place
>   in a noisy world,
> The perfect getaway,
> far from the buzz of traffic. (vv. 4–5 THE MESSAGE)

King David knew his internal posture was crucial to his external progress. His closeness to God would determine his clarity in being led. He understood being committed to God's House would help him better build his own house. David chose to not just follow God, but to build a life that would always have close proximity to His presence. He chose to leave the noise of the traffic that surrounded him and surrender daily at His feet. I love how King David—even as a powerful man—was so purposeful about his posture. He did not presume God would give him special privileges; rather, he pursued God's presence. That hunger caused David to not just know God, but to be called a man after God's own heart (Acts 13:22).

Our postures should not be accidental or casual when it comes to our relationships with God. In the middle, your posture can either propel you or imprison you. Your internal position will affect your disposition and in those middle moments, when we feel tested in our direction or challenged by the company around us, we need to commit again to being God-followers first. We must not allow weariness or disappointment to alter our positions, nor allow gaps to appear between our devotion and direction. David, in the midst of all his responsibilities and the demands of his kingship, chose to build a life that had a feetfirst posture, which means in our journeys it is entirely possible to do the same.

> FAMILIARITY CAN **CAUSE US TO** RECLINE IN A PLACE WHERE WE SHOULD **BE BOWING DOWN.**

OVERFAMILIAR

A feetfirst posture is best demonstrated in John 12, where we find the story of Jesus, Mary, and an alabaster box.

> Mary took about a pint of pure nard, an expensive perfume; she poured it on Jesus' feet and wiped his feet with her hair. And the house was filled with the fragrance of the perfume. (v. 3)

Here, amid a room of disciples, this woman entered and brought with her an offering for Jesus. As she walked into the room, the disciples were reclining at the table (v. 2). Yet Mary did not come to recline; she came to worship! Her actions would later challenge the posture of many in that room.

Familiarity can cause us to recline in a place where we should be bowing down. Familiarity can also cause us to become more concerned with what's on the table than who's at the table. The disciples that day failed to see that their familiarity was affecting their following ability. As this woman went to Jesus' feet, they began to feel uncomfortable and even became critical of her extravagance in their presence. However, what they failed to see was that her sacrifice at His feet was preparing Him for the moment He would give the ultimate sacrifice and lay His life down for His friends—friends who were at the table with Him.

Sometimes our closeness to something or someone can impair our discernment. The disciples were the closest to Jesus and yet they failed to see the significance of the moment they were sharing with Him. They were unaware that the next place their following would take them was to the foot of a cross. But this woman had purposely come to bathe those feet that later would be wounded for her sin. We must never become familiar followers, overlooking what we have because we are so preoccupied with what we don't have. Mary's sacrifice and worship in that moment became a posture check that some were very uncomfortable with.

SELF-SERVING

But one of his disciples, Judas Iscariot, who was later to betray him, objected, "Why wasn't this perfume sold and the money given to the poor? It was worth a year's wages." He did not say this because he cared about the poor but because he was a thief; as keeper of the money bag, he used to help himself to what was put into it. (John 12:4–6)

Often the ones who feel the most disturbed around "feet-first" people are the "Me First" people. The Bible says that Mary's sacrificial giving annoyed Judas. Judas was a "Me First" person, and Jesus knew that Judas had his own self-serving agenda. But it is not until the arrival of Mary's act of surrender that Judas's posture was clearly exposed to everyone present. At the sight of her generosity, he speaks up and accuses the woman of being a poor steward because her actions are wasteful and frivolous.

I have found "Me First" people will always try to tell you that living "feetfirst" is a waste of time. Unsettled by the ease at which you give, believe, or step out, these selfish folks can become a huge distraction. Disapproving of your devotion and trying to calm you down, they may belittle your actions and minimize the importance of your decisions. Yet Jesus, in that moment, spoke up for Mary and silenced Judas by reminding the disciples what true following requires.

OFTEN THE ONES WHO FEEL THE MOST DISTURBED AROUND "FEETFIRST" PEOPLE ARE THE "ME FIRST" PEOPLE.

Our follower-ship is strengthened when we worship and fix our eyes on Him. Don't ever apologize for your alabaster-box decisions. Don't downscale your passion or weaken your worship to fit in. Worship helps close the gap in moments we may not fully understand. It allows God to speak through our sacrifices. This kind of posture changes atmospheres and draws the attention to what really matters. Never be embarrassed to lower your posture so He can become higher. It is when we come to our knees that we see the path much clearer. "Feetfirst" followers always place Christ in front and commit to follow His lead rather than try to take the lead.

So what about you? What's your internal posture? Is it helping you to progress? Is it allowing you to see and hear clearly? Is it placing you feetfirst into His presence? On my own journey, though my heart was right in some situations, my direction had become wrong. I was too busy *doing* things for God. I needed a posture-realignment moment for my future so I could begin to see where I had lost Jesus.

You may have become so engaged in everybody else's priorities that you can't feel His presence. You may be so far forward in your venture that you can't remember the last time you sought His voice or drew on His word. Maybe you need to get back to the place where you seek first His kingdom and trust Him with all that other stuff.

Every day I have the same routine. I start each morning with a four-mile run. I do this for many reasons. It is good for my health, but it has also become essential to my wholeness as my daily "feetfirst" moment. It is where I remind myself whom I have decided to follow. I pray about all that lies ahead and ask God to guide me. I pray I will hear His voice and be mindful of Him, and that in the middle of the many things He will be my main thing. I encourage you to find your space—a place where you can focus each day on your following. It doesn't have to take long, and it doesn't have to involve a run. It just requires a willingness to surrender and place Jesus at the center of it all.

NO TURNING BACK

So let's go back for a moment to our disciples who started their whole ministry on the basis of the words "Follow me." They let their spirits lead, and they left the safety of the familiar to begin an adventure with Jesus that no handbook or job description could have prepared them for. Their journey was far from problem-free. It was a path that went through many middle moments where the disciples faced their own struggles with the direction they where headed, the doubts they faced, or the cost of the call. They, like us, discovered that following cannot be based on feelings, but must be based on faith. I am certain there were many times when the disciples wondered why they had said yes to that invitation to follow. There were many moments in the midst of doubts, persecution, trials, and tests that they thought about turning back. What began with an acceptance to follow Him sometimes became a daily renewed commitment to keep following Him.

Following Jesus can be uncomfortable and, at times, we may not even understand the direction He is asking us to take. We may feel there is little instruction for something that requires so much involvement. Therefore, the ability to surrender our many questions and be satisfied in His presence is one of the most important and beautiful gifts we can give ourselves. An attitude of worship can help your life keep moving past where your moodiness or emotions try to confine you. When we move our worship from a service once a week into a way of life, it allows us to continually place His presence over our problems, magnifying the Miracle Maker above the mess that may be in our middle.

The fragrance from Mary's worship covered His feet and clung to His garment, and it became a gift to Jesus in the most agonising middle He would have to face—the cross. Her "feetfirst" moment became a miracle in Jesus' own middle moment as He fought hell for your freedom and mine. The worship we bring in our middle is some of the very best. It costs us more, and therefore means more. But it also has the ability to give strength to another's struggles and to speak peace into their pain. Mary's worship was not wasted. In fact, it became a gift we are still learning from today. So however hard the road you are traveling may be, decide again to follow Him with a posture that, even in your middle, will not be moved. Follow as a true disciple would—with no turning back.

ACTION POINTS

1. Examine who is leading whom.
2. Adjust your posture to enhance your progress.
3. Commit to reconnect in the areas where you have lost Jesus.

PRAYER POINTS

1. Surrender again to following Jesus.
2. Pray to change any "Me First" areas to become "feetfirst."
3. Seek His presence over your problem.

THREE

KEEP YOUR SHOES ON

THE DAY STARTED OUT WELL FOR THE DISCIPLES. THEY HAD front-row seats to what would become one of Jesus' most memorable and preached-about miracles—the one with the ever-expanding lunch box in Mark 6. Jesus feeds five thousand men, plus women and children, from one boy's fish sandwich. This was one of those days when it was a dream to be a disciple. Let's face it: there were many days when the twelve had more than their fair share of challenges—when they were kicked out of town, persecuted, or tested for being on Jesus' team. But this particular day was a *great* day. On this day, Jesus taught the masses, healed individuals, and blessed and encouraged many. As daylight was fading, Jesus, always mindful of others who still needed help, informed the disciples it was time to move on. Scripture records that He turned to His disciples and gave the following instructions:

Immediately Jesus made his disciples get into the boat and go on ahead of him to Bethsaida, while he dismissed the crowd. (Mark 6:45)

GO TO BETHSAIDA

One thing I have come to discover about following Jesus is that when He says "go" He means *go*. Jesus doesn't get slowed down by past miracles or the last great event, He is always moving forward in search of new places to bring life and hope. Too often we want to camp at our victories and build monuments for our successes. Yet the disciples had learned that Jesus came to start a movement, not build a monument. When Peter appealed to Jesus to stay on the mountaintop at the place of transfiguration in Mark 9, he asked if they could set up camp there. Jesus' response informed Peter He had no intention to stay on the mountain when there were thousands in need back down in the valley. I love this about Jesus. He doesn't stand still for long. He is constantly

JESUS CAME TO START A MOVEMENT, NOT BUILD A MONUMENT.

moving forward, always intentional in His direction to go and reach more disciples. We need to learn this same lesson. We have to be careful that we are not tempted to stay on the shores of our successes or overstay our welcome in the places of our breakthrough. Instead, we should be aware of what still lies ahead.

Jesus knew the crowd that applauded Him one day would be the same crowd that would jeer him the next. Therefore, He never got caught up in the performance trap because He was called to a life of service, not success. Jesus was not in need of people's approval, which meant He was always able to pursue the purpose for which He was sent. He lived immune from peer pressure and was ever mindful of bringing His Father pleasure. If you are following Jesus, His continual pull to help others should inspire you to steer away from distractions—good or bad—that will try to hold you back. Following Jesus will keep you free from building altars and seeking audiences. It should keep you mindful of the cause and indifferent to the applause.

Jesus' pace was not altered by people's responses. He did not linger for the fans or try to avoid the critics; He just did what He was destined to do, which was one of the life lessons Jesus wanted to teach His disciples. Therefore, on this particular day in Mark 6, He did not allow the disciples to overstay their time on the shore where a miracle had taken place. He did not want them to build a monument honoring that moment. He was too aware of the people in the next place awaiting their miracles, so He told His disciples to get in their boat and head to the next shore.

KEEP YOUR SHOES ON

The word *immediately* in Mark 6:45 lets us know just how committed you have to be to follow Jesus. We have to build lives that have enough flexibility to go, move, and act as God's Spirit leads. *Immediately* doesn't allow time for us to overthink or doubt the directions. It requires great faith and commitment to keep moving forward.

Sometimes when I take my children over to a friend's house

to drop something off, I will warn them beforehand that we are not staying. I ask them not to nag me to stay when we get inside and tell them ahead of time that this will be a quick visit. Yet so often, no matter how strong my warning, once we arrive and they see their friends, my instructions disappear from their minds and they make the mistake of taking off their shoes. Very quickly our plans are jeopardized as they begin to get comfortable. Where before we were just stopping by, now they have settled in for the night. At this point, I have to stand on the doorstep and plead for them to come and put their shoes back on so we can leave.

I think Jesus faced the same type of dilemmas with His disciples. He had to remind them at various points, "Don't take your shoes off. We're not stopping here for long, so don't get comfortable." Notice how Jesus didn't ask the crowd to move on to Bethsaida, because it was not the crowd that had said yes to His "Follow me" invitation. The same is true for you and me.

IT CAN BE IN THE FAMILIAR THAT WE MOST STRUGGLE TO FOLLOW.

Jesus doesn't want to convince reluctant disciples to follow Him; He wants us to be willing and ready for His "immediately"— which means keeping our shoes on. When we signed up for this great adventure, we also said yes to some great expectations. When we say, "Yes, I am all in. I want to follow You, Jesus," He takes this as our surrender to allow Him to set the agenda— which means that you and I will always have to be ready, at any time, for the next "immediately."

Jesus gave the disciples some instructions to follow. They

were not complicated, and He was not asking them to do something they were incapable of. The instructions were to get in a boat and row. They were fishermen; they knew how to row a boat, and they knew the town of Bethsaida. Jesus was asking them to follow Him by doing something that was very familiar. But it can be in the familiar that we most struggle to follow. On the shore where the spectacular is happening, there will always be a crowd. The Jesus on the shore doing miracles—that's a Jesus who is popular to follow. Everyone wants to be with Him on the miraculous days! But the Jesus who says, "Get in a boat, row it yourself, and go where I tell you to go"—that Jesus will take a whole new level of follower-ship. If Jesus had told His disciples that they were going to be anointed to levitate to Bethsaida, no human effort required, they might have been more excited about this opportunity. But being told they had to do something very ordinary after they had been involved with something so extraordinary was not as appealing.

The middle is where we can give into "I don't feel like it" emotions, and it is often the place delays or excuses will attempt to frustrate our following. After a long day, the disciples had to push their boat out onto the water, with just the instructions Jesus had given them. And to top it off, He was not even going to accompany them for this part of the journey. The life of a Jesus follower requires us to do the same, no matter how we feel. This place, the familiar, is where we are most tested. It requires following Him in our devotional times and prayer lives, in the discipline of our choices and our commitments, and in the familiar of our churches, marriages, relationships, and resources—even when we don't feel like it.

SAFETY CHECK

On a recent flight to the U.S., the air steward began giving the usual safety briefing and suggested we, as passengers, check the safety information card in the seat pockets in front of us. Since I fly regularly, I had heard this talk hundreds of times and so I chose to ignore the advice and not even look at my safety card. As I was happily daydreaming through her talk, I glanced to my left and watched as the woman two seats over from me sprang into action. She got her reading glasses out of her bag and began to not just glance at the safety sheet but digest the information it offered. She looked up and down the plane, checking the exit information and ascertaining where the features it described were situated. At that moment I thought to myself, *I am so glad this lady is sitting in my row; we are all in good hands.* Clearly we were going to be a lot safer because of her due diligence. I am reminded of that as I sit and write these words to you. Your application of the information you read will not just help you through the middle, but also provide security for all those who are traveling with you. Let's not become disengaged in the middle with the very truths that we may at some point need to stand on in order to secure our futures and those of the ones around us. It is in the middle we typically find out how well we listened to the safety instructions while still on the ground.

When the crew on board a plane takes every passenger through the safety demonstration, they don't envisage there will

> FAITH IS SOMETHING WE ARE SUPPOSED **TO GROW NOW,** BEFORE THE PROBLEM HITS.

be any need for the oxygen mask to drop from the compart-
ment above your head; nor do they think you will need to use
the cushion underneath your chair as a flotation device. But just
because they don't see a problem doesn't mean they won't prepare you for the problem. They know if a disaster struck, the
panic in the air would not be conducive to learning the lesson at
that time. They don't want to wait for the middle of an air disaster to let you know how the equipment you are already sitting on
works. Understandably, they would rather teach you the lesson
while you're still on the ground.

The same is true when it comes to God. Too many times we
can have a false idea of what faith looks like. We tend to doubt
people's faith if we see them prepare for adversity. But faith is
something we are supposed to grow now, before the problem
hits. Jesus gave Joseph a dream that led to Pharaoh storing up
crops for the famine that was coming. He helped him with a plan
for the Egyptian economy so they would have supply when the
lack came. God was giving Joseph a preflight provision check,
and Joseph was listening. His attentiveness allowed him to prosper at a time when many others were panicking. Joseph's wise
council not only saved his life, but it also enabled thousands of
people to benefit from his faithfulness.

FREQUENT FLYERS

For many Christians, we can become frequent flyers in our
relationship with God. We are so used to hearing sermons on
faith for the valleys and even have refrigerator magnets display-
ing the promises of God. We buy bookmarks, posters, T-shirts,

and journals with verses that speak of His power and faithfulness. But just because we do something often does not make us experts. For example, since I married an American who is a diehard Seahawks fan, I often watch the NFL, but I couldn't tell you how to play or even what the rules of the game are. I listen to music in my car and hum a lot, but I have no clue how to read or play music. I may give both music and football some attention, but I give neither any devotion. Attention lets the information pass by, but devotion takes the information and makes it part of my life.

As believers, just because we hear a truth doesn't mean we have secured that belief into our hearts. Just because we give it some form of attention doesn't mean it has our devotion. And, therefore, the danger is we become frequent-flier attenders but never attachers, passive listeners but never aggressive actioners. We have many frequent-flier miles in loving God, but our many miles have not thrown us into deeper waters with God. Instead, they have moved us into nicer lounges.

I have many miles with several airlines, and the reward for my customer loyalty is shown in increasing luxuries, better waiting rooms, nicer food, and more choices. I get to board the plane faster and check in more smoothly. Believe me, I love having some of those perks. But all those perks will mean nothing if the aircraft I boarded was involved in an accident. The air disaster would treat me no differently, whether it was my hundredth flight or first flight. In that moment, I would realize the lounge could not save me but the safety information could have.

We need to make sure the frequent-flier miles we accumulate as Christians are not just so we can access the better lounges or be entitled to more perks. We cannot afford to allow our familiarity with God's promises to replace our fervency to believe in them. We must not get so familiar with God's Word that we don't feel the need to study it any longer. We cannot snooze in our seats on Sunday and then expect to fare well in the storm that may be brewing on Monday. We have to listen differently, act quickly, and realize that what we think we already know all too often is the very thing we don't know at all.

BUILD IT YOURSELF

I have never been the best person at following instructions. I don't know how to read a map or operate the electrical devices my kids seem so capable of. And when it comes to flat-packed furniture, forget it! Not long ago I went to IKEA for a set of dresser drawers. I was in a rush and found one on a shelf that seemed to fit the requirements, so I put it in my shopping cart and headed to the exit. At the cash desk, a very unfriendly clerk asked me what I was doing. I explained I was buying the set of drawers. She proceeded to tell me I had to go to Aisle G, Row 24, for those drawers, as what I had in my cart was an already-built unit for display purposes only. I inquired about what I would find in Aisle G and she said it would be a box with instructions on how to "build it yourself." I didn't like her suggestion at all, so I persisted in asking if I could take the assembled drawers that I had already loaded. Her face told me I better go to Aisle G or she would call security.

My problem was that I did not want to have to build something using the instructions. I wanted it to already be made. But if I wanted to have the desired piece of furniture, I was going to have to go to Aisle G, Row 24, and build it myself. The same principle applies when we follow Christ. We may occasionally have the blessing of something that has happened due to a God-intervention or provision. But the more we follow Him, the more we find that He will send us to Aisle G time and time again—as He wants to teach us, not do everything for us.

God has given us so many instructions to help us build our hearts' desires. If you ever wonder where those instructions are, I suggest you pick up your Bible and start in any aisle! You will find He has left plenty of instructions for His disciples—both past and present—to follow. The word of God is our ultimate instruction manual, with directions on how to steward our money, run our homes, love our spouses, manage conflict, deal with doubts, raise our kids, have self-control, and love others. And the more we build from this book, the more we look like the Manufacturer of this manual. The problem is that too many times we don't want to read instructions, so we put up with poorly constructed marriages, faltering faith, or broken beliefs. We try to take someone else's life off the shelf and copy that model to save us the time and effort. However, God, like that cashier in IKEA, is not denying us the item we want to build; He is just not going to let us take a shortcut. He won't give us a display model. He will, however, teach us how to do it ourselves. Then we can help instruct others when they need to build those same things to furnish their lives.

HE WANTS TO TEACH US, NOT DO **EVERYTHING FOR US.**

I sometimes look at the way we do life as Christians and wonder how many of us are building from God's instructions and how many are trying to copy, or even borrow, another's faith to survive. I didn't like what the cashier was telling me, but I had two choices: either leave with nothing, or leave with the resources I needed to begin. I don't want to borrow someone else's joy; I want to discover how to find my own. I can't try to copy someone else's gift; I need to unpack what God has gifted within me. I can't take someone else's ministry or lifestyle; I have to follow the instructions on how to build my own home and family. God is not saying no to your desires, but He is saying, "I have instructions for you on how to do this well; they're on Aisle G, Row 24."

THE PERFECT STORM

The disciples in Mark 6 were given some very clear instructions of their own. As they boarded the boat and began to row, they knew they had to meet Jesus in Bethsaida. They pushed away from the crowds and onto the calm waters while Jesus went to the mountainside to pray. Then something very interesting— but, we will come to realize, not surprising—happened. Just as they rowed their boat away from the shore where they had been with Jesus, headed to where they were told He would meet them, a storm began to break.

> Later that night, the boat was in the middle of the lake, and he was alone on land. He saw the disciples straining at the oars, because the wind was against them. (Mark 6:47–48)

I love how the Bible records such detail for us to glean from. In these verses, we can see how the trouble that was about to surround the disciples did not happen at the shore but waited until they were in the middle of the lake. This was the "perfect storm" sent at a time when it could cause the most confusion. The enemy, who knew the significance of the middle, timed the storm that seemingly came out of nowhere to rock the disciples' boat—and their faith. The same thing happens to us on our journeys—the Devil will often hold off the bad weather until we're headed to the middle.

Why the middle? Because there is something that the enemy knows about the middle that we need to wise up to. He has discovered that the middle is when we enter the change zone, which for the Devil is a danger zone. He knew when the disciples took one stroke past the middle of the lake that they would be closer to Bethsaida and meeting Jesus than they would be to their pasts and the shore they left behind. He had a vested interest in not letting that happen. The middle is also a defining point. The enemy wants to try to stop us from taking one more step forward. He wants to keep us on the other side of the breakthrough, closer to our pasts than our futures. So when he sees that we are about to go through the middle, he stirs up the perfect storm.

IT IS IN THE MIDDLE OF THE STORM THAT WE DISCOVER WHAT IS IN THE MIDDLE OF US!

In the middle is when we are at the most vulnerable point, too far away from the last shore to reach back for safety and not close enough to the next shore to grasp it. In the middle the test is internal, while all the challenges are external. But that's why Jesus had given them such clear instructions. All they needed to do was remind themselves of the last thing He had said to steady their spirits in the storm. Jesus had been clear: "Go to Bethsaida. I will meet you there." The turbulence we face does not alter the instructions He sends. Don't miss this point: it is in the middle of the storm that we discover what is in the middle of us!

WEATHERPROOF

Shortly before dawn he went out to them, walking on the lake. He was about to pass by them, but when they saw him walking on the lake, they thought he was a ghost. They cried out, because they all saw him and were terrified. (Mark 6:48–50)

This next part of the story may surprise you, but the more you follow Jesus the more you come to realize He is never going to do what you expect Him to do. As the story progressed, Jesus' followers suddenly found themselves in the storm. They quickly moved from peace to panic as they likely felt, possibly even expected, that Jesus owed them an intervention. But the Bible says Jesus saw their distress and was simply planning on passing them by. Jesus was going to walk right past the disciples, who were freaking out in the boat. He had no intention of stopping in the storm. Jesus—kind, gentle, grace-giving, their friend, teacher, Lord—was choosing to walk on when they were freaking out. Why would Jesus do that? Did He not care or not see the disciples drowning in the middle? Jesus was all too aware of their problem, but He did not intend to stop, as He wanted them to become more aware of His provision. He had already given them some instructions, and all they had to do was follow them.

Jesus was their guarantor. Isaiah 55 tells us:

So is my word that goes out from my mouth:
It will not return to me empty,
but will accomplish what I desire
and achieve the purpose for which I sent it. (v. 11)

If Jesus tells you He is going to meet you at the other side of the lake, then He will not stand you up. He has no panic or fear when the weather changes, because His word is weatherproof. The turbulence does not change the instructions; the wind does not cancel out His Word.

You can choose to ignore the instructions and try to make it on your own. Or you can save yourself time and keep on going until you get your promised result. One thing you can be sure of is that the instructions on that paper will never change. The instructions are set, and if you trust the Manufacturer, you can trust the instructions. The instructions are not given to you to try to control you.

THE TURBULENCE DOES NOT CHANGE THE INSTRUCTIONS; THE WIND DOES NOT CANCEL OUT HIS WORD.

They are there to guide and help you on your journey to get you to the place that was promised. God's Word never changes. You can choose to ignore the instructions or you can choose to follow them, but either way they will remain the same.

We live in a time and day when, sadly, many people break their promises or vows. Vows that are made with great ceremony and emotion are short-lived as reality hits and the commitment seems to cost too much. Maybe in your career you were promised a promotion or pay raise that never happened. Or in the relationship that promised forever and fidelity, you now face betrayal and brokenness. Though we live in a world where people's promises are flawed, we must be careful that we do not allow that mentality to seep into and adversely affect our trust in God. If we don't prevent past disappointments from contaminating our present situations, even though we know God is greater, our expectations will be so much lower.

In the middle, our levels of trust are tested. Jesus' behavior in the middle of this lake can seem rather uncaring, almost as if He were teasing the team who trusted Him. Why would He walk by the ones He loved when they were so clearly scared? The best picture I can use for this is something that many of us who are parents can relate to with our own children.

WALK ON BY

In England, children start high school at eleven years of age. (I know . . . crazy, right?) Recently, our daughter, Hope Cherish, turned eleven. So this meant moving up to a different school. Not only would she suddenly be in a much larger environment, and hanging out with kids up to the age of eighteen years old, but she would be traveling to school each day by herself. For the past eight years, we had taken Hope to a small, idyllic school along the waterside, just down from our house. It was a school Hope and her brother would ride bikes to every day in the summer. But going to high school meant leaving this routine behind. Though everything in me wanted to drive her to high school, and escort her inside (and if they would let me, even wait outside all day to collect her), I had to realize she would never get to where she needed to be if I was always going with her. She needed to learn how to get there on her own. My job, as a parent, was to give her some great guidance and instructions for her to follow.

The first day of high school came around. I went with Hope as far as the bus stop, and we waited together for the bus to arrive. We had rehearsed the drill—how much her fare would cost, which stop to get off at, and so on. In England, we have no school buses, so she entered at the deep end. She was riding a regular commuter bus filled with many people on their way to work. I watched as she fumbled for her change at the bus conductor's pay station and as she searched the bus for an empty seat. I waved good-bye and then fought the urge to jump in my car and follow the bus to school. I needed to allow her to figure this out for herself. There would be times when I would be away and she was going to have to do this without me, so we needed to start the practice of getting to and from school on her own now. I did not make Hope get on the bus alone because I didn't care. I did it because *I did* care. I knew she had to find her own way.

I remember that first morning when my phone beeped and the text message landed. "I made it, mum, off to class now. I love you, Hope." Of course she made it! She had trusted me and followed the instructions. Hope was growing up, and my "walking by" that day was allowing it to happen. It was only one week later that my previously nervous daughter was now staying after school for tennis club and sports class and getting her own way back and forth from every meeting. Why? Because she had learned in that moment that what she feared was actually not that frightening, and what she doubted, she was more than capable of doing.

Jesus knew the exact same thing was true for His disciples.

He knew He was not always going to be there in the manner they were becoming used to. He knew when He was gone they would have to trust what they had been taught and stand on what was promised. He knew He couldn't come and settle every storm; they would have to learn how to steer through them on their own. He was going to walk on by because He loved them enough to do so. You have to trust, when Jesus sometimes walks by you, that it is not that He doesn't care, but instead that He cares enough to let you figure out some things for your own sake.

ACTION POINTS

1. What instructions do you need to follow?
2. Where do you need to replace panic with peace?
3. What do you need to change in the middle?

PRAYER POINTS

1. Pray for strength to get to the next shore.
2. Pray God's weatherproof word into your storm.
3. Resolve to build it yourself.

FOUR

STRAINING AT THE OARS

HAVE YOU EVER STRAINED A MUSCLE? IT'S NOT A NICE FEELing. The moment it happens, you can feel the pain of the muscle pull or the ligament tear. It is then that you realize you've overstretched or overextended your body in a way that it was ill equipped and unprepared to handle. A bad strain is painful physically, but it is no less painful when it happens emotionally or mentally.

On our journeys through life, we will inevitably come to places where our abilities and faiths are stretched. But with every stretching point comes the potential for a straining point. Straining is rarely pretty and never looks professional, and yet it is part of the process that we so often have to endure when we are moving from where we are to where we are called to be. God never promised our journeys would be smooth sailing; in fact, He said just the opposite, guaranteeing trouble ahead.

John 16:33 tells us, "In this world you will have trouble. But take heart! I have overcome the world." Therefore, if we are guaranteed that straining points are coming—challenges not just felt by us but often witnessed by others as they journey alongside us—then maybe we should give a little more time now to building stamina for the storm that surely lies ahead.

STRAINING POINT

The disciples were between two shores when they hit their straining point. Having just left Jesus and the multiplication miracle of loaves and fishes, they were now halfway to the next shore—Bethsaida, where He had instructed them to go and where He would come to meet them. "He saw the disciples straining at the oars, because the wind was against them. Shortly before dawn he went out to them, walking on the lake" (Mark 6:48).

All of a sudden, in the very middle of this lake, the strain began to unsettle the sailors. The wind and the waves gathered momentum, and what had previously been a peaceful paddle for the disciples was fast becoming a stressed-out straining session in the middle. Where before they had paid little attention to how they were rowing, now they were gripping the oars and trying to steer the boat to a safe place. In that straining moment I am certain conversations became more tense and fear began to grip their hearts. Undoubtedly, their facial expressions changed as they found themselves pressing hard against the wind, using the oars to cut through the turbulent waters. The disciples went from serene sailing to strained rowing.

WITH EVERY STRETCHING **POINT COMES THE POTENTIAL FOR A** STRAINING POINT.

In the middle our lives can suddenly change. In one moment we can be paddling along in our parenting; then suddenly a crisis happens with one of our children, and we find we have to increase our strength and deepen our strokes to make it through the unforeseen stormy seas. We can be rowing along at a great speed financially, and then we are hit by a circumstance, a storm that changes our resources, and now we are rowing to survive. That sudden shift in the middle happens to each of us in many different ways; nobody gets to avoid it. It's simply part of the process of life—which is why we need to learn how to handle straining points before the storm hits.

SYMPTOMS OF STRAIN

WebMD, a medical website, lists the following symptoms of a physical muscle strain: muscle swelling and tearing, pain while at rest, pain in a specific area, and weakness and an inability to move. At one time or another I have experienced all of these symptoms in my own body, as I am sure you have too. Strained ankles, a strained neck, or a strained back can cause a lot of discomfort and alter how we are able to move about. Similarly, our spiritual equivalents—like a strained faith, strained relationship, or strained peace—can go on to have much the same symptoms.

When I have allowed adverse circumstances to cause stress to my faith, I have felt those symptoms. Weakness, agitation, and an inability to progress can happen just as quickly in the spiritual as it does in the natural. An offense untreated becomes a stumbling block to the future. A hurt that is not allowed to heal hinders our progress, and a sin that is hidden, rather than forgiven, will add stress to future shores we may set sail for. What begins as a small place of stress can grow until we reach the point where our faith and feelings are totally out of joint.

A surface wound can be easy to identify and, therefore, treat. But a strain can be a lot more complicated to remedy. With the pain often hard to pinpoint and not visible to the naked eye, it can take much longer to correct. In the spiritual, we face the same complications with strains often being well hidden. That is, until we reach the middle. The disciples were not just physically feeling the strain that day as they battled the storm on the lake; they also felt the strain in their faith as fear entered their hearts and panic overwhelmed their minds. They thought Jesus was a ghost on the water! They doubted the direction they had been certain about earlier and questioned their ability to make it through the middle to reach Bethsaida.

Spiritual strain is a serious condition that far too many people live with day in and day out. In order to get back the full mobility God has intended for us, we need to be willing to take some of our faith muscles back to the gym.

OUT OF SHAPE

Years ago I had an aversion to any form of physical activity and was very out of shape. On one particular occasion, when my husband and I were in the U.S., I learned just how out of shape I was. As a treat to ourselves, we had booked a few days in a beautiful lodge up in some very snowy mountains. When we arrived we found ourselves overwhelmed by the scenery and the enthusiasm of all the other hotel guests. They told us stories of the mountains that we needed to go discover and coerced us into snow skiing. As I had never skied before, and Steve was a great skier, this didn't feel like either a safe or a fair suggestion, so a compromise was made. We agreed to go for a day of cross-country skiing instead, which I was told involved nothing more than gliding along some well-worn tracks. We set off with great enthusiasm. The scenery was breathtaking and the weather perfect. After an hour, with both of us high from the mountain air and the excitement that I had managed to stay upright the whole time, we decided to go a little farther. That was the beginning of a very bad decision. Four hours later, exhausted and freezing, we returned to the lodge. We had taken a much longer trail than we had planned, which resulted in navigating hills and terrifying bends we were not expecting to encounter. Because I was a novice on skis, I screamed and fell down a lot more than any person should—especially on what was supposed to have been a romantic and relaxing getaway.

When we finally arrived back at the lodge, all I wanted to do was get out of my snow gear and find some more comfortable footwear that was not attached to skis. We had about an hour to get changed before our dinner reservation, so sensing some aches and pains from the day's robust activity, I went up to the room to run a hot bath to soak in. Exhausted and waiting for the bath to fill, I laid down next to my husband on the hotel bed, where we were both glad to simply be still. As we laid there we began to feel muscle spasms. In the next ten minutes, we would go from mobile to completely unable to move as our strained muscles seized up. The next few hours in that hotel room would have made for the most hilarious scene in any comedy movie, as both my hubby and I had such bad muscle strains we couldn't get off the bed. Steve had to literally roll and push me off the bed as we realized my bathwater was running over. But because I couldn't walk to the bathroom, I had to crawl there. I pulled myself across the floor in an attempt to turn off the taps.

We had to cancel our dinner reservations as neither of us could get up, let alone sit up at the restaurant table. So we called room service instead. When the waiter came with the food to the door of our room, we shouted from the bed to come in and then asked him to lay the food on the bed between us. Though he followed our request, this shocked server looked very concerned for our sanity. Over the next two days, we did not leave that room as we nursed the aftershock

WE NEED TO ENSURE IN THE MIDDLE THAT WE HAVE THE STRENGTH TO HANDLE THE STRAIN.

of our strained muscles. The only people we saw were either the maid or room service, both of whom had to navigate around our lockdown situation. A mere four hours on skis had resulted in well over forty-eight hours on our bed in absolute agony. We had both taken on a physical challenge that we weren't ready for. In the exhilaration of our cross-country marathon, we had no idea just how much damage we had done. But after the skis were off, we found we were living with a strain that would change the rest of our mountain-lodge vacation.

My physical condition was not ready for the challenge I had taken on, and my body reacted in a way that let me know it was not prepared for the stress I had just placed upon it. The pain from that one afternoon's activity stayed with me for a long time, and even now, the suggestion of going on any kind of skis triggers bad memories of hours of aching muscles and sleepless, painful nights.

The reality is that the enemy has a vested interest in not just making your middle miserable, but marking you in a way that you carry that pain for far longer than you would have to if you had been spiritually ready for the challenge. He wants to use middle moments to alter lifetime callings. He wants to take the strain and exaggerate its pain. If he can't sink you, he will almost always try to leave some permanent strain in your spirit that will seek to limit you. We need to ensure in the middle that we have the strength to handle the strain. The reason I felt so much pain after my skiing debut was because I was unprepared. But if I understand the middle will create straining points, then I can prepare now to strengthen those points, If we know in the middle our core beliefs will be stretched, why can't we start building them up now? The strain is coming, but how long it remains depends on our ability to build spiritual flexibility.

REPETITIVE STRAIN INJURY

When we don't deal with the source of a stress or strain, and continue to repeat the same pattern causing the tension, we allow the development of a repetitive strain injury to occur. This is a condition that is on the rise in our twenty-first-century world, as many more people spend all day at a computer or at a desk putting repeated pressure on a particular strain. Yet as believers we, too, can develop the same syndrome. We don't need to allow the pain to repeat or the stress to compound. Often, we find the storm passes but the strain remains, revisiting us in many different ways as we continue on our journeys. If you have strained trust it will be tested, strained forgiveness will falter, and strained love will fail to last.

Over the years, I have seen great potential be held prisoner by past pain. I have seen the lesson that was meant to be learned be relived too many times. When one relationship fails it should not mean that every other relationship that follows is doomed to the same end. However, if we refuse to face our failings, hide our hurts, and allow the residue from one broken relationship to jeopardize the future of another, then we will increase the potential to repeat the pattern—developing repetitive strains in our souls.

As a pastor, I have watched people enter our church after being through various storms in a previous church. They come seeking a new shore. They want a place to leave the past behind them and move on. But even though they have found a new place, they can't enjoy the freedom it wants to give them because they have kept some of the strains from their past. When an area in which they felt previously mistreated or misunderstood is mentioned, the strain can be seen in their nervousness to commit or their hesitation to trust. The stress from the past has the power to shrink the possibility of the present.

The storm is often the place where the strain occurs, but it's long after arriving to the next shore that the strain's effects can be felt. The disciples strained at the oars as they tried to row against the wind and waves, but the real muscle ache would come when they woke up the next morning on the shore. Their arms would be aching and their shoulders would be tense from the struggle they had tried to row through. Only when they were at rest would they realize they had caused some muscle damage.

As you read this chapter, pay attention to your straining muscles, the places where the dull ache is hiding and the aftermath of a storm has left its toll. It is time to heal the hurts from your strain in the middle so you can be fully ready for what's ahead.

COMPOUNDING INJURY

It's not enough to just make it through the middle; we also have to make sure we deal with any damage caused while we were there. You can ignore the strain, but ignoring it will only compound the injury that will eventually catch up with you on your journey. The strain you ignore becomes future pain that you delay. So today, learn to recover from a strain. If you strained your faith, fix it; if you strained your relationship, resolve it; if you strained your courage, rebuild it.

Several years ago, I had to navigate a storm I didn't see coming. A close friend left the church we had been a part of for a long time together. The departure left a lot of hurt and misunderstanding. I found myself in the middle of an emotional storm, yet I didn't realize just how strained I had let my heart become. It wasn't until months after the storm had passed that I noticed I had adapted a strong aversion to any mention of this person's name. If the person was referred to, the hurt would scream out on the inside of me and I would end up saying something negative or critical. Rather than starve the pain, I fed my strain with social media updates on this person. As I went about compounding the injury, I also went about containing my own destiny.

I am ashamed to say it took me a long time to realize the

only way to be free of the strain was to deal with the source. To ask forgiveness and to humble my heart, instead of hollering my hurt. After I went back to fix the strain, I suddenly found new muscles for my journey. And when the next middle moment came with a hard-to-navigate person, I had built the right muscles to have the right response. These decisions in the middle become part of our miracles. They give you the gift of being able to heal quicker and bounce back faster; they give you flexibility in your soul so you don't have to become frozen in time.

As an avid runner, I run several miles every day. I love the space and exercise it gives me, but a few years ago I strained my knee. Instead of fixing it, I ignored it. After all, it was just a small thing. However, after running on this strain for so long, I discovered the small ache became a large problem, and I now required a supportive brace to be worn over my knee to run. The damage I should have repaired had become a much bigger problem. Just

THE STRAIN YOU IGNORE BECOMES FUTURE PAIN THAT YOU DELAY.

as this happened to me physically, it can spiritually. The strains you ignore don't go away but can become compounded as you keep running through life. And the more distance you run untreated, the more damage you can cause. Then all of a sudden, one day an injury surfaces and sets you back years, because you have not taken the time to settle the strain. You may even be in a season that is, at the moment, relatively calm. But your peaceful season does not mean you are necessarily in peace. Even though the storm is over, the strain may still be very present.

BITTERNESS AND BARRENNESS

Michal, David's wife and the daughter of Saul, deeply loved David. Their relationship had been through many testing middle moments, and in those moments, Michal's love and commitment to David had become strained. David had hurt Michal's heart, and this heartache began to bury deep into Michal's soul. Unwilling and unable to bring healing to her pain, she allowed the injury to become more and more stressed, as she saw everything David did as a repeat strain to her situation. When David was happy, it increased her bitterness; when he was doing right, it strained how she felt she had been wronged. Though her strain was silent, its voice was heard through Michal's actions. And because she didn't deal with it, the deep offense stressed the strain that eventually sabotaged her future.

In 2 Samuel 6, we see David returning to Michal and their household on a day that is cause for great celebration. It was the day David was bringing the ark of the Lord home! He was bringing the blessing of God to His people! And yet, as David came into sight, Michal—who was watching the parade of worship and thanksgiving from her bedroom window—began to let her strain speak. As she saw David dancing before the Lord, her hidden hurt became visible hate. She said to David:

> "How the king of Israel has distinguished himself today, going around half-naked in full view of the slave girls of his servants as any vulgar fellow would!" (v. 20)

So often the strains we gain in the middle surface at the most inappropriate times. At the times for great acceleration, those unattended offenses will cause great devastation. It was the sight of David's success that aggravated her pain. She was bitter at his blessing, and her bitterness would eventually cause her barrenness.

> David said to Michal, "It was before the LORD, who chose me rather than your father or anyone from his house when he appointed me ruler over the LORD's people Israel—I will celebrate before the LORD. I will become even more undignified than this, and I will be humiliated in my own eyes. But by these slave girls you spoke of, I will be held in honor." (vv. 21–22)

David's response was not to defend himself or to try to prove his right to celebrate the return of the ark of the Lord. But, rather, David went straight to the origin of the strained muscle and addressed her hurt. Knowing the history of her relationship with her father, Saul, and her unease at David's prominence in her father's presence, David refused to fight the symptoms and instead spoke to the source. He spoke of the unspoken resentment between her father and himself, and her jealous spirit that refused to acknowledge God's choice of king.

This outburst led to Michal's barrenness. Her small strain became a huge sabotage to her future. Don't ever underestimate small strains, because they can have huge ramifications. If you are unsure where the strain is in your life or relationships, watch how you respond in different scenarios. Watch how you react to someone else's success; watch out for the jealous eye or the critical comment. Watch how you read social media and watch your comments on peoples' posts. Don't allow the strain to speak.

Watch how you react to the things you don't approve of, and be careful not to judge or condemn because of your hidden agenda. Watch how you handle those who have mishandled you, as your future, like Michal's, is so often exposed in those moments when you allow your strain to speak. Though Michal may have had cause for upset, she had no case for perpetuating or publishing the problem. She may have had her feelings hurt, but now her feelings were being allowed to hurt not just David but all those in her household. For Michal, the choices she made in the place of strain led to barrenness. Yet for others in the Bible, they used their straining points as launching pads for even greater significance. Instead of getting bitter, they became better. In the place of strain, they found seeds for success.

FORGIVENESS AND A FUTURE

One of those stories is found in the life of Joseph. Joseph took the pressure point of prison and turned it into a training place for the palace. He would not allow the stress of his injustice to shape the success of his future. Even when he was reunited with his brothers, instead of having a repetitive-strain-injury moment, he forgave them and changed not just his relational future, but also the future for his family. He had every reason to feel offended by his brothers. These were the very people who left him for dead and lied about his whereabouts to his father. They had betrayed him, sold him, abused him, and betrayed him. Their actions put him in the middle of a fierce storm of testing that led him to prison. But instead of letting the strain sabotage his future, he dealt with the source of the pain. He determined not to allow this straining point to become his finishing point. Instead, he used his time in prison to learn a lesson: to deepen his trust, not his pain. He grew in a place of confinement and he prepared for his next shore.

In the middle of his storm, Joseph used a straining point as a spiritual workout for his soul. When he was finally face-to-face again with the ones who had hurt him the most, he spoke; but nobody heard strain. Instead they heard love and grace. He didn't allow the strain to prolong the pain and neither should we. You have too much to do—more people to reach. God wants to use your life, so don't let the past sabotage your future. Don't allow the strain from the storm to wash up on your next shore.

DON'T ALLOW THE STRAIN FROM THE STORM TO WASH UP ON YOUR NEXT SHORE.

If we accept that we are all going to have times when we need to strain at the oars, then why don't we decide now to get working on the muscles we will need to navigate those waters? Where is your spiritual muscle weak? Where do you need to strengthen your core or stretch your faith? What investment could you make *now* for the middle that is coming *later*? Where do you need to, once and for all, mend the strain? Where do you need to call time on the nagging ache you have lived with for far too long? Where can you remove the pain from your past that is damaging your present?

When I need to get some muscles straightened out, I head for a deep tissue massage—where I allow someone to work on all those knots hiding under my skin. Maybe it's time for you, too, to get some deep-tissue mentoring in your life, so surround yourself with company who will deal with the knots others want to avoid.

Allow yourself to be vulnerable enough to let the Spirit get to work on the repetitive strain that you keep agonizing over. We all need to build our lives so they are strong enough for the strain, stop straining at the same places, and learn the lesson and get more muscle to ensure momentum. Work on your faith, patience, generosity, temper, and confession—so you can now have a spirit that sustains you in the strain.

ACTION POINTS

1. What are your straining points?
2. What source of stress do you need to address?
3. How can you strengthen your spirit for the storm?

PRAYER POINTS

1. Pray for peace to enter the areas where stress has been present.
2. Pray for healing in the place of hurt.
3. Pray for freedom to move forward.

FIVE

THREE THINGS

SO HOW DO WE FIND PEACE IN THE STORM? HOW DO WE FIND God's voice in the void? In Mark 6, as Jesus began to approach the disciples' boat, they panicked, thinking they were seeing a ghost on the water. Jesus spoke three simple statements into the storm that had the power within them to restore order in their middle moment. Jesus' words became stabilizers in the storm and gave them the ability to readjust perspective and realign their direction.

Let's examine each of the three instructions given and unpack the help they hold for our own journeys. Jesus told the disciples to take courage, to remember who He was—"It is I," and to not be afraid.

> Immediately he spoke to them and said, "Take courage! It is I. Don't be afraid." Then he climbed into the boat with them, and the wind died down. They were completely amazed, for they had not understood about the loaves; their hearts were hardened. (Mark 6:50–52)

TAKE COURAGE

If something is available for you and me to take, then it is entirely possible that we could leave the very same thing unclaimed. Jesus said, "Take courage"—which meant courage was a choice the disciples could make. We learn from an early age that our lives grow in correspondence to our courage. Whether it is finding the courage to walk rather than crawl, or to say yes boldly rather than a safer no, it's the courageous decisions that remove our limitations. Yet many times we wait to feel courageous before we take action. We must realize that the feelings may never come, but the choice is always available for us to act upon. Jesus knew that a courageous leader was within every disciple; He knew it when He first called out to them, "Follow Me." He knew it when they followed Him to the places where they were persecuted. He saw it when they were rejected, mocked, and marginalized. Jesus wanted to remind the disciples to stop looking at what was around them and seize what was already within them.

IT'S THE COURAGEOUS DECISIONS THAT REMOVE OUR LIMITATIONS.

One of my favorite films growing up, and still today if I am honest, is the classic story *The Wizard of Oz*. This is a film where four unlikely friends embark on a dangerous journey to each attain a gift they deeply desire. Dorothy, who has run away from her family, longs to go home; the Tin Man wishes for a heart; the Scarecrow desires a brain; and the Cowardly Lion seeks courage. On their journey, as they follow the yellow brick road, they face all kinds of tests and trials: fighting an army of Winged Monkeys, taking on the Wicked Witch of the West, and traveling through the frightening Dark Forest, to name a few. As the four friends travel down this winding yellow brick road full of unexpected dangers, they are so aware of what they believe they lack that they fail to see all they have gained. They do not realize that the gifts they are going to ask the great Wizard to give them they already possess. On the journey, the Cowardly Lion displays great courage as he fights to defend his friends from the witch's army. The Scarecrow, who assumes he has no brain, masterminds a plot to enter the fortified palace and free Dorothy. And the Tin Man proves he has the largest heart of them all.

Near the end of this childhood classic, the four friends realize the Wonderful Wizard of Oz, who was supposed to help them, has no special powers at all. All the Wizard of Oz can do is affirm in each character what he or she already has within. So the Wizard gives the Cowardly Lion a medal of courage for the bravery he has displayed; he gives the Tin Man a heart-shaped pocket watch to remind him of his kindness; he gives the Scarecrow a diploma to celebrate his wisdom; and Dorothy finds out that the ruby red shoes she has been wearing from the very start of her journey are all she ever needed to take her back home.

Our journeys with God will often lead us to the same discoveries! Second Peter 1:3 tells us that God has already "given us everything we need for a godly life." What if we were to live as though we truly believed those words? How much more courage would we take when we realize just how much we have been given? Yet we doubt what is within as we compare and contrast our journeys with others, feeding our inadequacies and starving our courage. Jesus knew the disciples had the strength for the struggle, but they failed to look within to find what was needed to face what surrounded them. Today, maybe you are in your middle and God wants to remind you of the same truth. He invites you to put down the things that are containing you and pick up the courage within you.

WITHIN YOU

When I was a teenager I went to a bible camp where, in a meeting one night, there was a moment when people were asked to go forward if they wanted prayer for healing. I was sitting in the back row of the crusade tent, when the person next to me asked a question I wasn't prepared for. She explained how she had twisted her ankle days earlier and couldn't walk properly, and this was why she was sitting in the back of the tent. She wanted to go forward for prayer but wondered if it made more sense if she just asked me to pray for

BE MORE MINDFUL OF WHAT YOU HAVE RATHER THAN WHAT YOU HAVEN'T!

her. She explained how the Bible said in Matthew 18, "Again, truly I tell you that if two of you on earth agree about anything they ask for, it will be done for them by my Father in heaven" (v. 19). I couldn't deny that her logic made sense, but in that moment I was overwhelmed with a feeling of inadequacy. I wasn't the leader, and everyone knows the anointing is much stronger at the front of the tent than the back row, right? She asked me again, only this time a little more persistently, so I found myself agreeing. *This*, I thought, *is sure to be a disaster.* To make matters worse, she rolled her jeans up to reveal her swollen ankle and said, "You start," as she closed her eyes to pray.

I stared at the obviously-fractured ankle and then closed my eyes, too. I partly thought, *If I can't see it, maybe it will be easier to pray for!* It was about sixty seconds later I suddenly realized all the things I had heard taught at bible camp were now going to be tested. I had edited in my mind the verse that said that God could use me; now my version read "God uses only the chosen few" and I was not one of them. I believed in His resurrection power but I did not think it actually resided at my address. As Romans 8 says, "The Spirit of God, who raised Jesus from the dead, lives in you" (v. 11 NLT).

If those verses were actually true, then I didn't need to go to the front for anything—I just needed to call on the Jesus that was within. I suddenly blurted out a prayer and took the courage to speak healing into this girl's ankle. No sooner had I finished praying, when the girl, who before had been limping, was up and jumping around. I don't know who was more shocked! I couldn't believe it was actually true; God could use me! All I had to do was make myself useful. I often wonder how many times God is saying to us in the storm: *Go ahead and take it! Take the joy; it's your strength. Take the peace; it passes understanding. Take the faith; it will silence the fear. Take the courage; it will calm the storm.* If God is telling you to "take it," He means it's there for the taking. Maybe it's time to be more mindful of what you have rather than what you haven't!

Jesus has done all He can do for you and me: the cross, the resurrection, the Spirit and the power of God residing within us. He has fought for our freedom, sacrificed for our salvation, and bled for our forgiveness. Now it is our responsibility to pick up. In the middle you need to learn how to pick up your promises, pick up your faith, and pick up His Word. Pick up the scriptures that have the power to change your situation. Take courage because He is your healer (Exodus 15:26). If you're in distress, pick up the promises because He is your peace that passes understanding (Philippians 4:7). In the face of past hurts, pick up that He is the restorer of your soul (Psalm 23:3). When facing bad news, pick up the truth that He is the One who makes all things new (2 Corinthians 5:17). Let the things that are intimidating you know that no weapon formed against you shall prevail (Isaiah 54:17), and that greater is He that is in you than He that's in the world (1 John 4:4). When the enemy hands you fear, take courage; when he gives you pain, take courage; when he surrounds you with darkness, take courage. I have found the more I take courage, the better I can navigate any challenge.

GOD'S FAITHFULNESS **DOESN'T ALTER** WITH THE WEATHER.

"IT IS I"

I love how Jesus announced to the disciples, "It is I." In their moment of disorientation, He wanted to focus them back on who He is. Jesus wasn't just a fellow passenger; He was Jesus, the One the Word promised would come, the Savior, redeemer Lord! "It is I," the One who heals the lepers and raises the dead. "It is I," the One who casts out demons and restores the broken. Jesus was affirming "It is I." "It is I, Jesus," and this present darkness has no power over Me. "It is I" who was in the disciples' middle, and the great news is He is in yours too.

RECALL

When my children would get scared in the night or have bad dreams, all I would have to do was walk into their bedroom, and not even turn on the light, but simply whisper, "It's okay. Mum's here." Without even opening their eyes, they would be settled by knowing the voice that whispered was a voice they associated with safety, protection, love, and peace. That voice said, "It's okay. It's me, Mum. You don't need to panic. I am here." Just as my voice comforted my kids in the dark, God's voice does for you and me. When we feel the conditions are harsh or the circumstances are dark, He reminds us of who He is. He doesn't need to do anything to prove "It is I"—His presence is enough.

When we face the turbulent tests in the middle is when we need to know how to harness the power of recall. Let's not be forgetful about who God is and all He has done. Let's not be blindsided by the test and forget the testimonies of our past, as they can become fuel for our future.

When I started dating my husband, more than twenty years ago, he showed me a journal he had kept since he'd become a Christian. It was his prayer-and-answer journal. In it he wrote down the things he was asking God to do or help him navigate through. He would write down some of the desires of his heart, and then in the opposite column, he would record each answer that he would receive. As I read it, I was amazed to see that in every column, without fail, where there had been an ask, there was a dated answer of provision. His faithfulness journal was something we adopted for our family when we got married and is something Steve still diligently keeps to this day. It reminds us of who God is and what He has done and, therefore, what He can still do. It gives us recall in the drought: that the rain will come; it gives us recall in the lack: that God is able to provide.

God's faithfulness doesn't alter with the weather. During the storm, when Jesus told the disciples, "It is I," He was saying, "Don't forget who is on your side, in your boat, and who will meet you on the next shore." Recall keeps our hearts grateful. And in the gap, when we are tempted to complain, it helps focus our faith.

The time we most need recall is in the middle of the storm. Recall today His goodness, journal His provision, and sing of His steadfast nature. The disciples only needed to recall what they had seen on the last shore, where Jesus fed thousands from a lunch box, to know that same Jesus was just as present in their struggle.

ANSWER THE DOOR

My cell phone rings, and at the other end of the call is a rather confused and slightly annoyed voice. It's one of the friends we had invited over for dinner. I had been wondering why the group was a little later than expected—obviously this phone call was going to bring clarity to their delay. I was slightly embarrassed, however, to find that rather than them being late, they had arrived perfectly on time. And for the past ten minutes they had stood in gale-force wind and rain on our doorstep with a baby on their hip, ringing the doorbell repeatedly with no answer. They had also sent three text messages to say "let us in," but only now had I heard their last resort—the phone call.

I wish I could say this was a one-off occurrence, but actually, it happens more frequently than I would like to admit. It's not that we are purposefully being rude or playing games with our invited guests—the problem lies with our front door. We live in a house that is high rather than wide, and it can be hard to hear the doorbell ring. It's a house usually filled with music, kids playing, a dog barking, and noisy conversations, all at once. Beyond that, our front door has a strange design in that there is no handle on the outside. So even if someone is invited, they cannot let themselves in; they are completely dependent on someone on the inside of the door to open it for them. I guess it's a good security feature, but the problem is that as much as it keeps those who are not invited out, it also keeps those who are wanted from coming in.

That front door has caused many frustrated and funny conversations between our friends and family, and on more than one occasion, we have looked into replacing it. But that door has also taught me some valuable lessons. Many times when I have been in the middle of a storm and prayed for an answer, I have refused or neglected to let in the answer that God chose to send. Like the disciples who thought Jesus was a ghost, I may not have recognized the answer for what it was.

Luke 11:9 tells us, "Ask and it will be given to you; seek and you will find; knock and the door will be opened to you." God is letting us know He will answer. He wants to send help to the front doors of our lives, yet we can be totally unaware of the answer waiting to be let in. Therefore, no matter the situation, we must believe that God is able and be expectant that an answer is being dispatched.

In Acts 12, a funny story unfolds involving a praying church and an imprisoned Peter. The church, in fear of further persecution, was praying for Peter's release. As Peter sat in his cell, God began to move in response to the church's prayers, but their inability to perceive the answer kept them from their miracle for a while longer. Praying is always the best response to the problems you face in your middle. Panic will sink you, but prayer will not only lift you, it will invite God to get involved. The church prayed passionately for Peter's release but didn't prepare adequately for God's response. Prayer will always trigger a process, much of which we will never see. Therefore, when we pray, we must remain attentive and willing to watch for the ways in which God may provide.

ORDER FILLED

Recently, I was at the Chicago airport with my daughter. We were between flights and she wanted to visit the Golden Arches. "Mum, can we just get some French fries from McDonald's?" she asked. We didn't have much time, so I replied, "That's fine, but we need to be quick." My daughter took the money and walked up to the counter while I kept an eye on our plane's status. Well, more than went ten minutes went by, and we were still waiting for French fries. So I immediately went to the counter to complain and find out what the delay was. The gentleman behind the counter asked me, "What number are you?" I didn't understand his question, so I replied, "I don't have a number." He explained, "When you place an order you get a ticket with a number on it, and when your number is called, you collect your food at the end window." I turned to my daughter and asked for her ticket, and sure enough, there was her number right on the ticket where he had said it would be. It quickly became evident that her order had been filled ten minutes prior, but she had failed to understand her part in the process. I apologized to the gracious gentleman who was now getting some fresh French fries for Hope, but I walked away having learned a lesson: you can't just place the order—you also have to keep checking the counter.

The same scenario is true with God. We so often stop looking for an answer because we don't see the activity we had expected. We feel our prayers may have turned up nothing, so disappointed by delay, we walk away. We stop looking for the answer and, instead, remain overwhelmed by the problem. The church had prayed for Peter's release and God had started a process. They couldn't see it, but it didn't mean it wasn't happening. Don't ever stop praying because you feel nothing is changing. If we believe God answers prayers, then maybe we need to have more faith the answer is being dispatched.

Peter showed up on the doorstep of the praying church. The answer was now at the door, and yet the answer was going to stay on the doorstep for a little while longer.

Peter knocked at the outer entrance, and a servant named Rhoda came to answer the door. When she recognized Peter's voice, she was so overjoyed she ran back without opening it and exclaimed, "Peter is at the door!"

"You're out of your mind," they told her. When she kept insisting that it was so, they said, "It must be his angel."

But Peter kept on knocking, and when they opened the door and saw him, they were astonished. (Acts 12:13–16)

DISTRACTED

The servant girl, Rhoda, went to the door. She recognized Peter's voice, though she failed to let him in. In the noise and the activity of the home, she gave more attention to what was happening around her than what was happening in front of her. Though she could have opened the door, she put more importance on telling everyone else who was at the door.

I have found that often the middle can be a place where a lot of distractions delay us from attaining our answers. The noise of the circumstance can overwhelm the knock on the door, and the many different conversations can confuse what is the more necessary communication. We can leave on the doorstep the "It is I" we desperately need because we are distracted by all the "who's who" in the room. Rhoda knew it was Peter, but recognizing his voice was not enough for her to open the door.

She took the information that Peter was at the door back into the distracted room. The verdict was not to believe her version of events, but instead to doubt and dismiss her. The very thing the room full of people had prayed for they were refusing to receive. In their minds, Peter could not be at the door this quickly. This was not what they had decided the answer was going to look like, nor was it happening in their belief timescale. They first dismissed Rhoda as being out of her mind, then when she persisted they tried to explain away what she was saying with their own version of events.

How can the church pray in one moment and then dismiss the answer the next? I guess the same way I can invite my friends over for dinner and then leave them on the doorstep. The same reasons Rhoda didn't open the door can be the same reasons I don't answer mine. I can think I hear the doorbell, but instead of answering I will ask someone else to confirm if they heard it too. If they dismiss what I heard, then I don't make the effort to check it out for myself. A distracted state of mind can delay you opening the door; a room full of doubters can delay answers. Maybe you need to check the front door of your faith; maybe you need to check that you have not overlooked your answer.

If I fail to answer my door when the postman comes to deliver a parcel I ordered, he will often leave a note in my mailbox informing me that he has taken my parcel back to the post depot where they will hold it until I redeem it. In your middle, don't let the help you need go back to the depot. Don't allow notes informing you of what you could have accumulated pile up. On the contrary, expect your order to be delivered, and be ready to receive it, because God's Word never returns void.

> *So is my word that goes out from my mouth:*
> *It will not return to me empty,*
> *but will accomplish what I desire*
> *and achieve the purpose for which I sent it. (Isaiah 55:11)*

FEAR NOT

"Do not be afraid" was Jesus' final instruction to the disciples. I am sure Jesus sensed their fear before He saw it on their faces. Fear is intoxicating. And once you begin to give it room it will seek to take over. It will try to turn off every light that hope has switched on and close every door that faith wants to keep open.

Fear is an enemy to your future. It will let you sink in the middle. It will let go of possibility and instead hand you problems. Fear multiplies the waves and jettisons the lifeboats. Fear makes you panic and lose your grip on the truth, which is why the enemy loves to peddle fear, because once you accept fear it is not long before fear takes control of you.

Our good friend Dave had a terrible fear of dogs that stemmed from an unfortunate incident in his childhood when he was bitten and chased by a neighborhood dog that was clearly having a bad day. So when we bought a dog it posed a problem. Before Dave would come over for the evening, we would have to put the dog into the garage and make sure he didn't escape, as the sight of this big, bounding animal made Dave extremely anxious. Though Dave was now older, and it had been a long time since a dog had bitten him, the fear of that incident was still resident in his mind. Our dog, Jake, was as soft and daft as any animal you could meet, but this was irrelevant to Dave. His fear had made this one incident an irrational belief that every dog was out to bite him. Over time, we decided that if any dog was going to be able to change this, it was our dog. So one evening, when our friend was over, we let Jake out of the garage. At first there was a very frosty reception, as being near our dog brought back Dave's bad memories. But over the course of the evening, Jake began to replace some of Dave's unspoken fears with his wagging tail and winsome face.

Over time, Jake and Dave became great friends—so much so that when Dave enters the room, Jake never leaves his side! If we're watching a movie, he sits at Dave's feet, but also follows him around the house. Dave and his wife now have a little boy, Jay, who knows nothing of the fear his father had. Jay boldly walks up to Jake, who is twice his height, and pets him on the head; he has such confidence he even sits on him. But had Dave not faced and beat his fears, his son might have had the same fearful nature handed down to him.

FEAR INFLUENZA

Fears are like a flu virus. They are so strong within us that we can easily pass them on to someone else. Jesus knew that the influenza of fear was gaining strength in that boat, so he spoke into the darkness it was seeking to bring. He told the disciples to refuse to let fear go any further. Fears need you to stand your ground or they will take you off your feet. You have to immunize your fears with actions of faith. You must silence and replace them with a confident confession and meditation that will develop faith in its place.

1 John 4:18 says, "There is no fear in love. But perfect love drives out fear."

When we are in the middle, we need to address fear. We can't ignore it. We need to challenge its mind-set and pull down its imaginations. We need to let our love lead us where fear would never permit us to go. I have met too many people who are in their later years in life and—like Dave—because of one incident somewhere on their journeys, they have never moved on. They may have faced one broken relationship, so the fear of another heartache has held them in the middle, where they fear commitment. They may have faced a business failure, so the fear of failing again has frozen their potential. They fear ever dreaming again of achieving anything, and they become content to live where they are rather than try to have the faith to move forward to a better future.

Fear will make up stories of how you will never make it. But Jesus spoke these words to His disciples: "Do not fear." The same goes for every follower of Jesus today. If we are going to follow Him to the next shore, we cannot allow fear to take the lead. You can't follow Jesus if you follow fear. Where do you need to hear God's voice today, telling you to not be afraid? Do not be afraid of failing. Do not be afraid of trusting. Do not be afraid of committing. Do not be afraid of giving. Do not fear.

The disciples could have begun to row back to the shore they had left behind, to the last place where Jesus was breaking bread and they were being celebrated, or they could have kept rowing and gone on to a new place where new stories were waiting to be told. In the middle, they had a decision to make. Were they willing to follow Jesus even when the fear was intoxicating? Were they willing to push

ALLOW THE MIDDLE TO STRENGTHEN WHAT'S IN THE MIDDLE OF YOU.

past the wind that was against them? They had to decide if they wanted to arrive more than they wanted to settle.

We have to make the same choices today. Just like the disciples, we have three things that we can choose to put into action now: we can take the words of Jesus and take courage, we can recall who is in the boat with us, and we can tell fear to take a hike. We can choose to pick up the oars again and keep rowing, because as the disciples would discover, Bethsaida, their chosen destination, was closer than they thought.

You, like the disciples, have more lives to reach on the

next shore, more people to help, new relationships to embrace, dreams to birth, ideas to initiate, words to preach, songs to write, families to help, and souls to rescue. So in the middle, keep moving, and keep the instructions in front of you. Allow the middle to strengthen what's in the middle of you.

ACTION POINTS

1. Where do you need to take courage?
2. Where do you need to affirm who is in your boat?
3. What is it time for you to pick up?

PRAYER POINTS

1. Pray that you would see what is within you that can shape the world around you.
2. Pray perfect love will cast out all fear.
3. Pray for the discernment to recognize the voice at the door.

SIX

DROP ANCHOR

I DON'T CONFESS TO KNOW A LOT ABOUT BOATS OTHER THAN they make me seasick. Because of that, I don't spend a lot of time on the water. However, on the few occasions that I have been out on a boat with friends, we've ensured before setting off that someone on the vessel was able not only to steer, but more importantly, to stabilize the boat. As much as someone needs to know how to move the boat forward, he or she also needs to know how to hold the boat steady. To that end, a seasoned sailor possesses the skill and knowledge to secure his boat with an anchor that digs into the seabed. The rule of thumb follows that the larger the vessel you sail, the bigger the anchor you will require.

When it comes to our journeys and charting the courses for our futures, we need the same approach. We need to know how to "drop anchor" into God, His Word, His promises, and His grace. All too often, it is not until we reach the middle of our journeys that we discover how anchor savvy we actually are. It is here we discover if our anchor into God is an untested theory or a living reality. The further we venture out, the stronger the anchor we will require; and the larger the life we want to live, the deeper the anchor will need to go.

ANCHOR SAVVY

Without the anchor, the crew has no way to ground the boat. In the face of hostile weather, they are unable to stay secure. Anchorless, they become vulnerable to drifting with every changing tide. An anchorless life can also be susceptible to the same outcome, so before we leave the shallows for deeper waters, I want us to become "anchor savvy."

The Bible says that hope is an anchor for our souls (Hebrews 6:19). When your soul faces turbulent conditions, hope will give you the ability to hold your ground. When you are frustrated about your future, you have a hope that can fasten your faith. Hope believes in the face of the unbelieving. Hope holds when our souls wants to let go. Hope establishes what hopelessness extinguishes. Every soul needs a hope anchor, and every sailor of that soul needs to know how to drop that anchor when necessary. So where are your anchors? And do you know how to use them?

In Hebrews 6:13 we read of the unchanging, unbreakable qualities of God's promises. We have to take every one of these immovable anchors with us on this journey. At times, we may have to jettison some things overboard, but we cannot afford to throw away our confidence in His promises. We all know that change is inevitable, and the weather in any season can be unpredictable the deeper waters you venture into by faith. But it's much more important to stabilize and to be able to touch the bottom with our beliefs. Once we are out in the middle, once the commitment has been made and the journey is underway, it is too late to realize we left our anchors on the shore.

I DO

Before I got married, I took a long time to work on my commitment anchor. If I was going to push out into a forever relationship, I wanted my vows to hold me in every season. I did not want a commitment that held only in the shallows; it needed to be strong enough for the storms too. I needed to know I had placed onboard my life a commitment that was weighty, one that had substance and strength. In order to do that, I knew I needed to make some room away from others to know this was what I wanted and what I was willing to work for.

I remember the time when I sensed my very dear friend, the man I had been dating, was getting ready to propose to me. To everyone's surprise I broke the relationship off for a week. I called a time-out. It was not because I didn't love Steve; in fact, just the opposite. It was because I realized how much I loved Steve and that we were coming to that "this is it" moment. I knew I was about to commit for the rest of my life! I wanted to step back and make sure that when I said yes I had an anchor of commitment to weigh in with all the emotions I was feeling. I remember that week being so hard as I isolated myself from the many voices I knew would encourage me to just say yes. But those other voices were not going to make this commitment. Only my voice would say "I do" to the vows spoken, so I needed space to affirm what would become a destiny choice. Thankfully, Steve understood what was going on. He gave me the space to sink my anchor deeper, as he also did not want to set sail with a reluctant partner onboard.

Though people may have thought I was unkind to take that time away from Steve, and maybe thought I should have been clearer at this point of our dating life, we are both glad I did. I was in my early twenties, and if I live a good, healthy life, our marriage is potentially an eighty-year union. When I said "I do" at the altar a year later was not the moment I dropped an anchor—for me it happened earlier. Today that same anchor goes deeper each year.

Anchors of any type of commitment or vow deserve the time and space they require to ensure they are securely attached.

> ANCHORS OF ANY TYPE OF **COMMITMENT OR VOW** DESERVE THE TIME AND SPACE THEY REQUIRE TO ENSURE **THEY ARE SECURELY ATTACHED.**

Ecclesiastes 5:5 says, "It is better not to make a vow than to make one and not fulfill it." It speaks of the process of making a vow, and warns this is something we should take very seriously. Don't be overimpressed with the big promise or the dramatic gesture. God isn't. A vow unfulfilled is like an anchor with no rope; it is a word that appears to hold weight but fails to ever attach. God sees and hears our vows as declarations of our intention and commitments to stay consistent, whatever the weather. These verses show that God is looking for anchors that will last. God desires that every vow made would be a vow kept, so we need to keep creating the space to ensure we can sustain what we are starting.

MAKE ROOM

Those who sail will tell you that in order to drop your anchor safely and securely, you need to first make some room around your vessel. You can't drop your anchor in close proximity to another boat, as ropes can get entangled and other vessels can get compromised. This also runs true in our spiritual lives. We need to detach from some things so we can attach to others. We need to make room away

TOO OFTEN WE ADD LAYERS TO OUR LIVES WITHOUT UNDERPINNING FOUNDATIONS FIRST.

from the interference around us, to establish our own beliefs and convictions so they run deeper than the surface of our lives.

How much room do you need to clear around you to drop anchor? You can't stand on the Word if you don't know the Word. You also can't claim the promises if you have never possessed the promise. The higher you want to build, the deeper you must dig. Too often we add layers to our lives without underpinning foundations first. Anchors are foundation fixers. They are the concrete in the commitment, the nonnegotiable amongst all the navigation. Without anchors, we can't hold our course and are doomed to a destiny of drift.

PLANTED

John 15 says if you remain in Him, He will remain in you (v. 4). Psalm 92 promises that our planting will lead to flourishing. Flourishing is a great attribute to have, yet both require great consistency. These two verses have become lifelong commitments for me and my family.

I was brought up in the same church that I now colead with my husband. I have had many opportunities to uproot. I have had times when I could have left from weariness, impatience, or hurt, but I have always chosen to stay planted. I remember when I went to university, moving to a new location presented me with an option to uproot. I had a reason for relocating and, thus, a valid excuse to be less involved. Nobody in my new setting would expect me to be in church. But I knew that my flourishing, in so many ways, had been a result of my being planted in the local church, and I didn't intend to start floundering at university. So while I was away, I found a church family and got into a small group. I also commuted back to my home church as often as possible to carry on serving and being involved. I still gave of my finances and kept to the values I had held for so many years prior.

To grow a flourishing life, consistency is key. In order for a seed to take root, it must be allowed time deep below the surface of the soil to become established in its new environment. Just as you would not keep digging up a seed to check on its roots, there are areas of our lives that we need to stop tampering with in order for something great to grow. The seed of my commitment rested in the soil of God's house for a long time before I saw the fruitfulness those decisions would later yield. I have stayed planted in seasons when nothing seemed to be happening. Being willing to stay accountable and teachable, I waited even when I felt like walking away. I learned my planting in God's house could not be based on the planting of others any more than their inconsistencies could cause my seed to be jeopardized. I did not want another's uprooting to uproot me too. My anchor went into God, not people.

I now have two children who are growing up in the church home I dropped an anchor into years ago. As they grow, they will have to decide if they want to establish for themselves this same commitment. I can't be the one who keeps them planted, and I don't want to be. I have met too

DON'T TRY TO HOLD EVERYONE ELSE'S BOAT AFLOAT.

many exhausted believers who have taken it upon themselves to be the anchor patrol. They run around from person to person, frantically trying to secure those who are prone to drifting. I have met pastors who are trying to drop anchors for their church members, or parents who are desperately attempting to anchor their rebellious teenagers into the youth program. Yet our responsibility is not to secure another's anchor. We can only take care of our own and pray that as we flourish, others would be drawn to our fruitfulness and seek the same growth for their own lives.

Teach your children from an early age how to find their own anchors into God. In your marriages make space as individuals to have your anchor of commitment secure. In friendships, don't try to hold everyone else's boat afloat. It will not only drain you—it could even sink you. We must all make room to establish the truths on which we desire to build our futures.

ANCHOR ATTACK

The middle moments of life are often where your anchor comes under attack. So knowing what you believe before the storm hits is crucial. What are your absolutes? What are the unchangeable truths you hold to in the midst of change? What are the commitments in the middle that will not be compromised? It is good to revise them frequently and confess them consistently.

For example, we have faced times as a family when we have felt, like the widow in Luke 21, that we had only two mites to give. But because we have an anchor about our giving, we have learned the amount is not what matters. It's the anchor of our commitment to sow in all seasons that God is interested in. Just as Jesus saw the value of the two mites over the value of the greater amount that others gave that day, God will always see those moments in the middle where you refuse to pull up anchors because of circumstance. Attitudes can be anchored, relationships can be anchored, promises can be anchored, commitments can be anchored, and your soul can be anchored!

In 2 Kings 4, there is a story of a woman who made some room in her home for the prophet of God to stay whenever he passed by. She had cleared some space so he could find rest when he was weary—a place to be refreshed from his ministry. Her provision of this space led to her being given a promise. The promise was that she would have a child! However, this God-fearing woman must have given up believing for a child many years before, as her response to the man of God revealed when he delivered the promise:

> "No, my lord!" she cried. "O man of God, don't deceive me and get my hopes up like that." (v. 16 NLT)

She pleaded with Elisha not to get her hopes up. We, too, can respond this way to the promises of God. We can become apprehensive about getting excited, in case we are later disappointed. We allow the thought of what could happen to dampen our faith for what God said will happen. This woman didn't want to hope for a child again; she didn't want to allow herself to become heartbroken. God is not trying to get your hopes up. He wants you to put your hope "down."

Hope is supposed to be put down into His Word and promises. Once your hope is down, you can give God more scope in your life. *Scope* is a term sailors use to describe the length of rope they attach to the anchor. The length of scope determines how far they can move from where the anchor is dropped. We need more scope in our lives. We need the type of faith that has enough rope attached to it that we can travel great distances without losing our stability and trust in God. For example, we can say we believe God is able, but scope asks us to step out in faith. We can say we are committed, but scope

> THE PLACES WHERE OUR FAITH IS MOST TESTED ARE THE SPACES WHERE WE HAVE TO GIVE GOD SOME SCOPE.

tests the strength of that commitment. We can say we forgive, but the offense will soon show how much scope we have attached to that anchor. The woman in 2 Kings said she believed in God, but now, through this promise, she was being asked to give God some scope to demonstrate that belief.

Once when I was young, on holiday, I went in a small, inflatable boat that was beached on the sand banks. I was happily playing, not noticing that the water had begun to rise underneath the boat. Before I knew it, I was floating in the middle of the water! I began to freak out, because even though I was in a boat that was designed to float, I barely knew how to swim! The further I drifted, the more my fear deepened, as the rising water highlighted my shallow swimming skills. The same thing happens for us with God. The places where our faith is most tested are the spaces where we have to give God some scope. Our challenge, then, is not to wait for the boat to drift before we learn how to swim. Don't drown in unbelief—take the places where you fear disappointment and begin working on your belief. And give God some scope.

CLEAR LINES

The woman in 2 Kings 4 did go on to have a baby boy. But as many of us can attest to, the arrival of the promise does not guarantee the removal of problems. In fact, sometimes it means the trouble can intensify. A few years later, the woman's son suddenly fell ill and died. The situation was as extreme as you could imagine. Now her real beliefs were going to be exposed. These middle moments would determine whether she was to sink or swim.

Verse 21 says that the woman's first course of action was to take the boy back to the place of promise. I love that in her most testing moment, she didn't panic but was purposeful. She didn't run around screaming or shouting about the boy's death, but she went back to the place where she had first made room to believe this promise was possible. She went to where she had allowed hope to sink deep. Too often in a time of pressure, we allow panic to disorient our destinies. We uproot when we need to stay planted; we jump ship when we need to drop anchor.

As a pastor, I have witnessed how devastating this can be. I have watched as problems have taken people not toward the promise, but away from it. Even those I thought wouldn't have allowed disappointment to dislodge them. But when it did, it also dislodged their family and friends who had placed their anchor in people instead of God. One person's upset, if handled poorly, can hijack many people's destinies, with his or her reaction rendering collateral damage. The woman in 2 Kings did not allow her son's death to devastate her whole family. Instead of running to her husband with the news, she made a plan to go back to the place of promise. Though this turn of events was unforeseen, her faith remained.

The story continues:

> When he saw her in the distance, the man of God said to his servant Gehazi, "Look! There's the Shunammite! Run to meet her and ask her, 'Are you all right? Is your husband all right? Is your child all right?'"
> "Everything is all right," she said. (vv. 25–26)

Though Gehazi tried to interrupt this woman, she would not even stop to explain the situation to him. She wanted to speak to only one person. She purposefully protected her conversations in her middle moment. She didn't need to add any doubt or distraction onboard when she was trying to stay afloat.

In the middle, whom we talk to and when we talk to them is either going to propel us forward or hold us back. In the middle of any turbulent season, we must learn which conversations to tangle with and confirm which people will deepen our anchors, but also understand what will disturb them. For example, if your marriage is in rocky waters, a conversation with the friend who is also unhappy in her marriage is not going to help you find your answer. You must refuse to be drawn into a conversation that does not help your conviction. If you are struggling with debt, don't keep talking to those who are drowning with the same problem. Whom you talk to at these fragile points is so important. And though this mother could have seemed rude to ignore Gehazi, and cruel to not tell the boy's father, she was taking her problem directly to the place of her promise. We must do the same.

BACK TO BASE

I used to play rounders—which is the English version of softball—at school. I really was not a great player, and typically I was the last choice of the team captains—whose job it was to choose their team's players. I was especially weak at catching, so I would be designated by my team to be a deep fielder, sent to where they didn't think a ball would ever reach (a place where I could do the least damage). I also wasn't a great hitter. But one thing I did well was run. I understood if I could run twice as fast as the others, even if my hit was weaker, I stood a chance of reaching home and scoring a point. My aim in the game of rounders when I was under hitting was to focus on one thing—running back

REMEMBER: FOR EVERY STOP YOU MAKE, YOU DELAY THE ARRIVAL AT YOUR DESTINATION.

to base. That practice often helped me score points when others failed. The same applies to our journey through the middle. When things don't look like they should, and when the situation seems worse rather than better, we simply need to stay focused on our faith.

We can score points against the enemy, not by trying to outsmart him, but by simply outlasting him. Determine to keep believing, keep praying, and keep going until you reach the promise. The woman in 2 Kings went back to base and the man of God who gave her the Word of God. She refused to be distracted on the way. Maybe right now in your middle, you are stopping at too many interim places, having too many intervening conversations. Remember: for every stop you make, you delay the arrival at your destination.

When Elisha eventually arrived to where the dead boy laid, he cleared the room so no one could interfere as he interceded. As he called on God, the boy began to respond and was brought back to life. Death and worst-case scenarios are no match for God's unchanging promises. He is able to bring back to life even those things that we feel are dying in the middle. He can restore and resurrect dreams and destinies, if we stay anchored in Him.

LION-PROOF

Proverbs 24:10 says, "If you falter in a time of trouble, how small is your strength!" I was always amazed when we played rounders at school with how those who had a powerful swing and could hit the ball out of the park could then be such terrible runners.

When the ball didn't go the distance they had hoped for, they didn't have the stamina to run the hit home. In the middle is often when you discover how strong you actually are. I have seen people who are strong in their vocations fall apart in the middle of problems in their families, and I have seen those overlooked as "weak" not falter for a moment when they were in the most testing of trials.

Daniel was a man of God who would not compromise his anchor of faith. He refused to change his commitment to daily prayer and devotion even when, as we read in Daniel 6, King Darius challenged it. By disobeying the king's orders, Daniel knew he would face persecution. Nonetheless, he refused to pull up anchor to avoid this punishment. Though Daniel's beliefs were tested, he did not allow the test to weaken his faith, but rather, he allowed it to strengthen his conviction. Daniel had a confidence that God was with him even when that looked like spending the night in a den of hungry lions. It was in the middle of the lions' den that the scope of Daniel's faith was revealed. Daniel, who declared God's faithfulness daily, was now being put in a place that demonstrated the depth of his belief. In the lions' den, Daniel's faith never faltered. We read that God took the lion that they all thought would kill Daniel and used it instead as a place for Daniel to lay his head for the night. In the middle of this most terrifying experience, Daniel trusted God. When he walked out the next morning, not only did he declare that God was faithful, the king decreed that all the people would call Daniel's God their God too. The middle tests our falter factor and always reveals God's faithfulness factor.

NOTHING WASTED

Have you ever persevered through something and at the end looked back and thought, *What was that all about? How can God have been in any of this?* You feel tested and weary; you have scars from the journey, and though you may have made it through, you still have questions of why this happened to you. Well, even here we have to give God some more scope. If we hold out a little longer, we will see how nothing is wasted in God's hands.

Going back to our story in 2 Kings, we could argue over why God would allow the woman's son to die. Why promise the woman a son she hadn't even asked for only for him to die and then be brought back to life? It seems to make no sense. In the same way, there are times in my journey when I have made it through the middle of a storm only to wonder what seed that storm could have ever held. So often, we write our own conclusions before God has even finished telling the story. And just as we may not see the anchor that's holding us steady below the wave, we can forget the never-failing promises that God has for us in the storm.

In 2 Kings 8, we see God was not finished telling this woman's story. He was working in the background. She built a life away from her own town for seven years because of a famine. Once the famine lifted, she returned home to reclaim some of her land and property. In order to make this request, she had to seek an audience with the king.

At the end of the seven years she came back from the land of the Philistines and went to appeal to the king for her house and land. The king was talking to Gehazi, the servant of the man of God, and had said, "Tell me about all the great things Elisha has done." Just as Gehazi was telling the king how Elisha had restored the dead to life, the woman whose son Elisha had brought back to life came to appeal to the king for her house and land.

Gehazi said, "This is the woman, my lord the king, and this is her son whom Elisha restored to life." The king asked the woman about it, and she told him.

Then he assigned an official to her case and said to him, "Give back everything that belonged to her." (vv. 3–6)

At the exact moment she entered with her request, God caused Gehazi to recall her story. The testimony from her middle was about to become the starting point for her future. Upon hearing her situation, the king was moved to restore to her all she had lost and to give her back even more than she even dared to ask for. God extracted seed from the sorrow and gave some meaning to her middle. Had she not gone through that storm, the king would not have heard her story that day, and the seven years of lack would have provided nothing but great loss. But here her most testing time, when her son died, was going to be the very thing God used to make sure she gained in a time of lack. This woman's story could have looked very different if she had uprooted, doubted, or allowed disappointment to disconnect her from the prophet of God and the promise of His Word. Because she remained anchored, her story continued. We must resist the urge to draw our own conclusions. We must not underestimate the seed God can extract from every sorrow as we remain in Him.

ALL THINGS WORK TOGETHER

All things work together for those who love the Lord. (Romans 8:28, paraphrase)

What I love most about both stories is how they demonstrate that when we hold fast to the promises of God, He not only works them out for our good; more than that, He proves that His promises stand fast.

The stories of Daniel and the woman in 2 Kings show how God had a better ending in mind than either of them could have ever imagined. Daniel became an even more influential leader, and this woman not only got her son back but also seven years' payback from the king. Your ability to stay anchored is key to your longevity. Going back to Psalm 92, it goes on to say: "They will still bear fruit in old age, they will stay fresh and green" (v. 14).

It speaks of planting causing flourishing, and then says that in their old age they will still bear much fruit. It's letting you and me know if we want to keep adding to our adventures, we need to keep dropping our anchors. If we want to make the most of our years, then we need to learn to strengthen our roots.

What are your anchors? Are they in God or are they in people? Where are you drifting? Maybe you need to add some anchors to your faith today. If so, make some space. Maybe you feel the testing on the line and it's time to let the stretch strengthen your conviction instead of weaken your commitment. Or maybe you need to untangle your line so that you don't feel the drag effect from the others you have allowed to bring you down. Allow God to help you extract the sorrow from your storm, and find the meaning in the middle to believe again that all things will work together for the good of those who love Him.

ACTION POINTS

1. Do you know where your anchors are?
2. Where can you give God more scope?
3. Where do you need to clear your lines?

PRAYER POINTS

1. Pray God helps you become anchor savvy.
2. Affirm and confess what you believe in your middle.
3. Pray with faith for all things to work together for good.

SEVEN

PIGGY IN THE MIDDLE

GROWING UP IN ENGLAND, THERE WAS A CHILDREN'S GAME that was very popular in every school yard. It was called Piggy in the Middle. I have no idea where that name came from or its meaning, but the game is very simple to understand and every child in England seems to know how to play it. It involves three players and one ball. Two of the players begin a game of "throw and catch" while the remaining player is positioned in the middle and tries to intercept the ball being tossed back and forth. Once he or she catches the ball, the player then gets to leave the middle, and the one who threw the ball swaps positions and now becomes the "piggy in the middle." This game is fun for a while, but eventually it can become frustrating— especially if you are playing with two friends who are much taller and who manage to throw the ball so high over your head that you are stuck in the middle for a very long time. Yet every player understands the rules: until you catch the ball you can't move position. So if you are in the middle, you have to find the determination and the perseverance to stay alert and keep your eyes on the ball.

In the middle of every situation, there is always a lesson to learn; there is a ball we need to focus on that, if caught, will change our future. If you forget playing Piggy in the Middle is about catching the ball, you could expend your energy running back and forth between the other players and getting more and more agitated that they won't move, when in fact it's not *their* turn to move, but *yours*. We, too, can transfer our expectation for breakthrough to the people around us in our middle moments. We can ask them to move for us or get frustrated that they don't seem to be helping enough. But the truth is they are playing the part they were assigned to. When you play your part and "catch the ball," others roles will be changed as well.

> THE MIDDLE IS NOT JUST **ABOUT BEING PATIENT,** BUT IT IS ALSO ABOUT **BEING PERSISTENT.**

I remember playing this game at school on many occasions. Rarely would I be able to catch the ball immediately. More often than not, it would take what felt like forever to intercept the play. The more weary I became, the more I didn't want to participate. As I lost the will to play, the less aware I became of the opportunities passing me by, any one of which would have allowed me to change the game. The middle is not just about being patient, but it is also about being persistent. It's not about waiting for someone to give you the ball; it's about knowing how to catch the ball. For those of us who are more passive than aggressive, this can be one of the most challenging parts of being in the middle.

STAND IN LINE

It is a well-known joke in my nation that when the British see more than two people standing next to each other, they begin to stand in a queue behind them, as they assume they must be waiting in line for something! We stand in line for our groceries, never thinking to complain at the ten carts in front of us or at the undermanned cashier points. We refrain from voicing our disapproval that the manager has put a trainee on the checkout at the busiest time of day. We will stand in line for hours at the bank to see a live person instead of having to deal with an automated machine. We line up for everything! I am married to an American who lives in England, so you can imagine the conversations—and at times, the confrontations—this has got us into.

My husband is on a single-man mission to stop the Great British public from being so passive. Most people actually end up thanking my husband when he takes up the challenge. At the grocery store, instead of waiting in the line, he goes and finds a cashier and asks the person to open a new checkout. At first, people may find his behavior a little forward, but it's not long before they are following us to the newly opened and much-faster-moving line. When we are waiting to be served or seen at the bank or doctor's office, and everyone is sitting in silence just watching the clock—you guessed it—my husband will go and ask questions. He will politely but firmly explain that people would be helped if they knew what the delay was for and how long we would all be kept waiting. He is definitely a guy who wants to shorten the time he spends in the middle, and that spirit is something I believe many of us need to harness!

Until you are frustrated enough to do something, you will

stay where you are. Until you find a passion to challenge the situation, you will remain a prisoner of the circumstance. Your life and mine, at any time, can enter a season where we feel like we are the Piggy in the Middle. If we can come to understand there is a ball here we can catch, we can change our places in the game a lot faster!

DON'T GIVE UP

The daughters of Zelophehad son of Hepher, the son of Gilead, the son of Makir, the son of Manasseh, belonged to the clans of Manasseh son of Joseph. The names of the daughters were Mahlah, Noah, Hoglah, Milkah and Tirzah. They came forward and stood before Moses, Eleazar the priest, the leaders and the whole assembly at the entrance to the tent of meeting and said, "Our father died in the wilderness. He was not among Korah's followers, who banded together against the LORD, but he died for his own sin and left no sons. Why should our father's name disappear from his clan because he had no son? Give us property among our father's relatives." (Numbers 27:1–4)

In Numbers 27, there is a story of five sisters, the five daughters of Zelophehad, who found themselves in the middle of a difficult situation. After the death of their mother years earlier, the girls' father brought them all up independently, and taught them how to work the land they would one day inherit. He empowered the girls to be confident and capable. And in the absence of sons, he trained them up to help him run the estate.

So when their father eventually passed away, the girls were prepared to take care of their land and steward the estate. Yet the law of their day denied the girls the inheritance their father had promised, as it documented that the estate could only be passed to a male relative.

Through no fault of their own, the sisters found themselves in this awful predicament. The future they had assumed was secure was now threatened and they were placed in the middle, dealing with their loss on one side and battling the law on the other. Sometimes the situations that create this kind of Piggy in the Middle setup are not of our own making; they are the unexpected eventualities life throws at you. Like the sudden unemployment that comes at the same

UNTIL YOU ARE FRUSTRATED ENOUGH TO DO SOMETHING, YOU WILL STAY WHERE YOU ARE.

time as the unforeseen illness, or the business that fails while the marriage is struggling. In between these two circumstances, somehow you have to find your faith and plan your exit strategy. The sisters—in between grieving and potentially losing everything they owned—refused to sit down or give up. They began to focus on something they could do instead of the things they were told they couldn't.

The story goes on to show how these sisters decided to appeal against the laws they felt were unjust. Between them, they resolved to not just catch a ball that would change their middle, but to actually change the game for all the girls who may one day find themselves in that same position. They didn't allow their grief to overwhelm them and they refused to accept the status quo. They fought for their future. It was their land and what their father wanted them to attain. The girls planned a strategy to change their situation, and I suggest you do the same.

GET UP

If you really want to shorten the time you spend in the middle, you have to position yourself correctly. You might see those kids playing Piggy in the Middle, jumping up and down in the middle and throwing their arms as high in the air as possible as they travel back and forth in that space, positioning themselves for the best chance to make a grab for the ball. The girls in the story found in Numbers had to choose their position. They did not allow grief to choose their next move, nor did they allow the law to silence them. We, too, have to decide what position we will take on the court of our circumstances. When the challenge comes, are you up on your feet or have you sat back down? Are you positioned to make progress or have you given into the process?

Years ago, when my husband first came to England, he wanted to stay on after his one-year visa had expired, to serve as youth worker in the church we now pastor. We were still dating at the time, and I was still studying for my degree. Steve was told that with no marital status and an expired visa, he would not be considered for a renewed status. The advice he was given by the immigration department was to return to the U.S. immediately; but that answer was not what my husband wanted to hear—he believed he should stay. It was something God had put on his heart to do. We both wanted to be in the same country while I finished my degree, and neither of us felt at peace with the answers that were being presented to us. We found ourselves in this middle moment where what we wanted seemed to be out of reach. But as you know by now, one of my husband's great qualities is he is not easily deterred. So instead of giving up and accepting defeat, he got busy. He began to work in the space that we were stuck in and looked for any ball of opportunity he could catch that would change our situation.

For the next year, Steve went back and forth with solicitors and immigration lawyers, filled in paperwork, and prepared himself by gaining knowledge and understanding for his visa battle. Eventually, after two court hearings, we were told to not apply anymore or the case would be thrown out, and we would never get the opportunity to apply again. The lawyer said the only thing left for us to do was

ARE YOU POSITIONED TO MAKE PROGRESS OR HAVE YOU GIVEN INTO THE PROCESS?

to try to apply from the U.S. So instead of packing up in disappointment, feeling everyone was against us, or questioning if God was with us, we bought two airplane tickets and flew to the U.S. We changed our position in order to attain what we needed for the sake of our future as a couple.

After arriving in the U.S., we went to the embassy office in Chicago for our appointment. We had flown thousands of miles for this meeting only to get there and find out that someone had made a clerical error and the office was already closed for the day! You can imagine at this point how easy it would have been to give up. We were tired of the "no" responses, disillusioned by the lack of help, and discouraged by the negative things that kept happening. We even had well-meaning Christians tell us it was God closing doors, so we should just accept that we were not meant to stay together. This is another reason why you need to be careful of the voices that coach you in the middle. This was not their battle, so it was easy for them to comment from the sideline. But this was our future and we knew that God had put it in our hearts. We knew we needed to focus on the ball that we believed we had to catch, the ball that would change the whole game! So just like Zelophehad's daughters, we positioned ourselves against a law that made no sense to the promise we felt God had for our lives.

I will never forget sitting in that office. I said to Steve, "Well, that's it. We might as well give up. We can't do anything about this now." I was tired of the never-ending paperwork and opposition, but Steve was not about to give up. He said, "Charlotte, we are not leaving this office without getting this sorted out." He stood up, and in that moment I knew things were about to change. Within two hours we went from being told no one could help us, to leaving that office with a stamp in Steve's visa for an indefinite stay as a missionary in the UK. We had never even thought something like that was possible. We had only been asking for another year's visa, but because Steve refused to sit down, and refused to let the "no" shape his faith, he grew more skill in the middle and eventually caught the ball that changed everything.

When we left the Immigration Office that day, I remember my husband saying, "Charlotte, God's office is greater than any immigration office." Let's never let people or situations shrink our futures. We chose that day to fight for what we knew was right. Whether that looks like a visa battle or a health struggle, an injustice or a promise you know is yours to attain, you have to choose the position you will take. And because of the skills and relationships we built in the middle, we have been able to help many others navigate similar battles along the way. Our perseverance became someone else's provision, and yours can do the same.

WISE UP

Discerning when we need to speak up and when we need to stay silent is something we can spend our whole lives attempting to figure out. We, at times, speak with great confidence, and other times with nervousness. Sometimes we speak with too much haste, and other times we are slow to speak up. Finding out how to use your voice is a crucial part of mastering your middle moments. Giving too much airtime to the wrong confessions or conversations can damage what you have worked so hard to establish.

In the middle, our voices can be challenged, and our confessions compromised. Yet it is here that our words matter more, so we need to manage our mouths well. Be careful what you give your voice to. Be selective about what you will speak for. Not everything needs your opinion and not everyone should set the agenda for your words. In 1 Kings 3:16, two women who had a tragedy to deal with approached Solomon. Both women had had a baby, and when the babies were just days old, one of the women had a tragic accident that resulted in her baby dying. Unable to face her grief, the woman lied about which baby is hers. Now they were both claiming the living child.

Unable to settle the dispute, the women came to seek the king's ruling on their situation. They argued their case in his courtroom, each pleading her innocence and appealing for the living child to be given to her care. King Solomon found himself in the middle of their dispute; they made their problem his business. Often in the middle, we find people who will try to do the same to you and me. Though their cases may not be this extreme, their arguments are no less passionate. They come into your life to make their problems your problems.

BEWARE OF THOSE WHO WANT YOU TO BE THE UMPIRE IN THEIR CONFLICT OR THE REFEREE IN THEIR DISPUTE.

They want you to manage the messes in their middles. Beware of those who want you to be the umpire in their conflicts or the referee in their disputes, as what they are really asking is for you to be their Piggy in the Middle. Whether you are being asked to be a relational referee, or the judge and jury between warring friends and family, be very careful what you give your voice to.

King Solomon knew his voice held power; his verdict would change their future. Solomon was not going to allow his words to be used as their weapons. In this way, his response provides a lesson for us all. After hearing their complaint, King Solomon refused to get in the middle argument. He did not take sides in their dispute, but rather, he asked for a sword:

> Then the king said, "Bring me a sword." So they brought a sword for the king. He then gave an order: "Cut the living child in two and give half to one and half to the other." (vv. 24–25)

Solomon's response to the women shocked everyone in the room. Refusing to be drawn into the fight, he sought to end the conflict by using his words wisely. Solomon knew that if he said he was going to kill the living child, the true mother would speak up to save the baby, and that's exactly what happened. Solomon's refusal to take sides caused the real mother to speak up.

SPEAK UP

Zelophehad's daughters knew they needed to find their own voices. They couldn't ask someone to fight this fight for them. They had to learn how to be heard in a world that did not even recognize they had voices. Their culture silenced their opinions. They were not given the same weight and esteem as the men in their community. With no father or brothers, they had no man in their world who could speak up for them. They had to either stay silent or stand up for themselves. So often, we can rely on others to speak for us. We want those around us to fight the battle, to go on our behalf and deal with the confrontation or the

> SOMETIMES, THE ONLY **THING STOPPING YOU FROM GETTING YOUR** BREAKTHROUGH IS *YOU.*

opposition. We can feel intimidated and insecure, and those feelings can feed our sense of inadequacy. Yet these girls came to the realization that no one else was coming to speak up for them. If they stayed quiet, as the custom expected them to, they would also stay poor and lose what they had worked for. Sometimes, the only thing stopping you from getting your breakthrough is *you.* Your refusal to speak up can cost you your inheritance. Somewhere between the grief and the injustice, a conversation took place between these sisters that moved them to find their voices.

The decision to speak up led them straight to Moses' door. He was the one who would have the final say once they presented their case. I love that these women went to Moses, who once had to find his own voice too. If anyone could understand the strength it took for them to go and speak to someone who had more power and authority than them, for something that seemed like a ridiculous request, it was Moses! He could relate; he knew how it felt to almost allow insecurity and inadequacy to keep him from speaking. When God asked Moses to step in the middle for the children of Israel and go confront Pharaoh, he allowed fear to exaggerate his stutter and it almost became his stumbling block. He felt ineloquent in the face of someone so powerful, yet it was his voice (stutter and all) that God wanted to use to bring liberty to millions of people.

Awhile back, we went to a parent-teacher conference. After we sat with our daughter's teacher and went through all of our daughter's academic progress, the teacher looked at us and said, "I would also like to tell you how incredible Hope is. She has been a delight to watch in class." Pleased, I asked what it was the teacher was so impacted by. She said, "Hope will always speak up when things are not right." Then she went on to share how many of the children were being intimidated by a group of kids who had formed their own little gang. Apparently, they had tried to pressure Hope into joining their "cool kids club." The teacher explained how Hope told these seemingly cool kids that it was not cool to act that way. Then she invited all of the isolated kids to sit with her in class and to hang out with her over recess. At ten years of age, she had refused to be silenced by the bullies. And she didn't allow them to intimidate her with what might happen if she didn't join them.

We all have bullies to deal with on our journeys—the people who seek to shrink your future and minimize your dreams, the ones who hold the past mistakes over your middle moments. Even grown adults continue to refuse to find their voices, fearing the repercussions it may bring. But as God's children we can find the resilience and strength to speak up. Others need our voices; they need us to get in the fight with them, and they need us to change the game so that they can find their place again.

The funny thing is that Hope never told us about this incident. She never asked us to go into the school and deal with it for her. She had realized she had a voice, too, and by speaking up she had changed the game for her classmates. It's important we teach our children that they have a voice. I believe Zelophehad had taught his daughters how to speak up, and as they found their voices they gave new language for others to fight for their cause. Where do you need to speak up? Where do you need to not only find your voices, but also come to understand your value? Where do you need to understand that you have something to say and that you are the best person to say it?

POWER UP

Zelophehad's daughters learned to use the power that accompanies persistence. Many times, the ones who make it are not the most powerful or influential, the most gifted or qualified, but rather the ones who are the most persistent. They are not going to go home without what they came for; they are going to make sure they catch the ball.

As children, we are naturally persistent. Our curiosity usually enables our persistence. As babies, we are born with a desire to develop and to conquer milestones; we persist past the stage of crawling because we are envious of those who have discovered walking! Though we may fall down many times, our desire to walk encourages us to persist. After attaining that achievement, our curiosity for what is next to conquer—in this case a staircase—drives us to continue to persist so we can make it to the top. We persist until we discover how to break through safety catches and stair gates! We persist as children because we want to progress; we persist with the spoon so we can enjoy the food, and we persist with the forming of words so we can be understood. Yet so often, the persistence we harnessed in our childhood can be lost in adulthood. But the growth we need to experience is no less valuable. We may not need to persist up a physical staircase, but we will need to climb many mountains to get the view God has intended for our lives. We may need to persist to be heard and to gain our breakthroughs. Sometimes we fail to persist because we become less willing to fall. We allow the possibility of failure to keep us stuck in the same place for years! But if you are ever going to get through the middle of any situation, mind-set, or season of life, you have to rekindle your willingness to persist.

BLIND BARTIMAEUS

In Mark 10, there is a story of a man who had been blind all his life. He was known as blind Bartimaeus. Every day he begged at the side of the road for food to survive. He was seen by most as helpless, and by others as a nuisance in the town where he lived. He was used to hearing people pass him by, day in and day out.

He would sit in a world of darkness and be treated with a wall of silence. Through no fault of his own, Bartimaeus found himself in a place where he didn't want to be, but he did not know any alternative way to live. One day, he heard that Jesus was coming to town and decided he would not let that opportunity pass him by. Even though he was at a disadvantage, he planned to position himself near where Jesus would pass and use his voice to call out for His attention. So blind Bartimaeus sat there all day waiting and calling. The crowds ignored him as if he were invisible, and it seemed Jesus was never going to come his direction. No one was informing Bartimaeus of where Jesus was, or offering him help to move closer to His healing. And so he had to find the persistence to keep calling out the name of Jesus from his darkness.

Persistence is a key to possession. Eventually, after Jesus had done all He came to do, He was about to head out of town. It was at this moment—as He was making His exit—that He passed near blind Bartimaeus. Imagine if—due to feeling ignored and overlooked—Bartimaeus had gone home earlier that day. Imagine if he hadn't persisted until the very end of the day. His lack of persistence would have meant he would have remained blind forever!

Persistent faith is forged in the middle—it's the tenacity we discover when things don't happen in our predetermined timing. Persistence is a powerful weapon in our arsenals as believers. When we use it well, it can make a huge difference. For Bartimaeus, it changed his situation from staying stuck as the blind beggar to receiving sight and independence for his future. What if your persistence meant the same? What if by persisting to get what is yours in God, you could move from defeated to victorious, from living in darkness to being surrounded by light? It's so easy to think your situation can never change, but the truth is it can all change. We just have to keep persisting.

CHANGE YOUR NAME

Blind Bartimaeus was tired of being defined by his deficiency. His name was Bartimaeus, but the place where he lived, his middle, was what defined him. He was labeled with his disability and was tired of being known for what he believed God could change. Sometimes we don't persist because we have become so used to the labels we have been given. We sit down wearing the badge of divorce, single parent, bankrupt business owner, college dropout, addict, rebellious teenager. They may be labels that describe a condition, but they are not supposed to be labels that become our definition! Bartimaeus was ready to drop the blind name tag, but he knew that in order to do that, he would have to persist past all the people who had called him that name for years. People who saw his blindness before they saw him, Bartimaeus.

Bartimaeus heard all the commotion in the final hour of the day and realized, *Jesus is here!* He knew this was his moment to change everything. He called for Jesus' attention, but the crowd around him told him to be quiet. They didn't approve of his boldness or his loudness! They reminded him it was not his place to call out to the Messiah in this way. But Bartimaeus was not about to let the crowd control his future. At every critical point, the crowds in our lives will become very opinionated. They will advise us, whether we ask for it or not, and they will let us know what they deem an appropriate response. But so often, our doing what is "appropriate" is what is extending our middle moment.

We need to let passion and desperation drive us forward, instead of allowing the status quo to settle us down. Maybe the situation you are in the middle of has been going on for years. Where before your passion positioned you, now the crowd has seated you. Don't become mediocre in the middle. Mediocrity says let's wait another year to change, let's consult more people, let's not be too hasty, and let's not upset anybody. The crowd was upset by Bartimaeus' boldness;

> **LET PASSION AND DESPERATION DRIVE US FORWARD, INSTEAD OF ALLOWING THE STATUS QUO TO SETTLE US DOWN.**

they were embarrassed by his expressiveness, but they were not the ones who were living a life of darkness and they were not the ones who were blind. Be like Bartimaeus and use your pain in the middle to fuel your persistence for a breakthrough.

CROWDED OUT

It's also important to be careful of the people who try to calm you down because your actions make them uncomfortable—people who would prefer you to be polite than get your promise in the middle. You need to listen for the ones who understand the burden of the blindness, who encourage you all the more to do all you can to recover your sight. Though the crowd was trying to calm Bartimaeus down, Jesus called him forth. His persistence captured Jesus' attention. In that moment, the same crowd who had been trying to silence him turned around to help him. The same people who told him, "Don't bother Jesus," were now taking him to Jesus. Crowds can be fickle, so don't base your behavior in the middle on the crowd's opinion. Go for Jesus. Call on Him and keep calling out until He stops and calls you forth.

Jesus asked Bartimaeus to move from his begging position and into a position where his belief could be seen. He told Bartimaeus to come to Him. Jesus did not go to Bartimaeus, He knew there was a breakthrough that would come in his willingness to push through. Jesus watched as this man who had called for Him all day pushed through the crowd. Mediocrity won't get you your miracle; mediocrity will leave you in the middle. The passion to persist will help you acquire your promise.

What is yours to attain today? What is that ball of opportunity you could seize? What partnership, idea, conversation, or connection awaits a change in your position? Focus your faith and be mindful of the role you have to play in your middle. Your miracle may only be one catch away.

ACTION POINTS

1. What ball do you need to catch?
2. Where do you need to find your voice and speak up?
3. What company do you need to leave to follow your future?

PRAYER POINTS

1. Pray to see opportunities around you.
2. Pray for the strategy to change your situation.
3. Pray for the wisdom today to help someone tomorrow.

EIGHT

RESPONSE TIME

A FEW MONTHS AGO WHEN I WAS IN THE U.S., I HAD AN unfortunate accident that ended with the emergency services being called. I don't remember the moment I passed out, but I do remember the moment I woke up. In addition to the noise and commotion of the ambulance, I was also surrounded by a whole cacophony of siren noises as a fire truck and a police car had also come to my rescue. Though I felt my accident didn't warrant that much attention, the rule for response to an emergency call in the U.S. is that whichever response unit is closest to you is the one that is to immediately make its way to the scene of the accident. In my particular incident, all three vehicles were passing through that part of town at that time, so all three came to my rescue. The firemen arrived first. I was promptly placed on a stretcher, put in the back of the fire truck, and rushed to the hospital. Because of the rapid response time of those on duty that day, within moments of my accident my situation changed from critical to under control.

At different times in life we have moments that require this same response, moments where we are at a critical place and our response time will mean the difference between avoiding a crisis and compounding the problem. We have moments where we can either exaggerate the drama or reduce the casualties. Therefore, if we are going to manage our middle moments with greater effectiveness, we need to learn how to become better responders.

If you were to look at your life today, how aware are you of your response time? How quickly, when it comes to the pull of the things of God, are you able to respond? What about when your life is in a crisis moment? When the unforeseen happens or the situation worsens? Is your response time effective or does it need some attention? The truth is that frequently in the middle our ability to respond comes under attack. We can find ourselves disoriented by the things around us and become less sure about the most appropriate response and actions that should follow.

FIRST RESPONDERS

When an emergency call is made, whoever gets to the scene of the accident first becomes what's known as the *first responder*. As the first to arrive, their response will determine what happens next. They are the ones who decide how to proceed, which treatment to initiate, and what set of instructions should be given to the people who follow them to the scene. First responders, therefore, need to be well trained and equipped to manage any and every situation they may encounter. A poor response by the first to arrive can mean a poor end result for all those involved. Just as those who are responding to an emergency call will have to work on their reactions, we, too, need to become better at first response moments.

In our journeys with God, it's often our initial responses that can propel us into the promises or hold us back from what's ahead. The response we have in those moments either strengthens or weakens our management of the middle. First responders know how to pack for every eventuality. They would never leave home without the medical equipment they know may be essential for survival on the scene. First responders are trained to know what kind of response is required for each call. Once the signal is received, the sirens are switched on and all other priorities are shifted. In that moment, their first response is not fear at what they may face, but a sense of readiness to help in the way they have already been trained.

We need to take time before problems arise to pack some answers. We need to roll up our faith for first-response moments, and be armed with a ready yes to the opportunities we may be asked to embrace. We need to check to be sure our bags are packed with enough love and grace, compassion and courage, so that when those moments happen we don't allow a wrong response to be the first on the scene. God wants to call our lives into new relationships and opportunities and take us into new territory, but on too many occasions our response can't embrace the future—as it is so strongly fixed in the past. If our first response is negativity, cynicism, doubt, or disappointment, this will set the scene for our next action. We can end up retreating when we should be advancing, and we can remain the same when we actually have an opportunity to change.

REACT OR RESPOND

When the apostle Timothy—Paul's young student in the faith—was getting ready for the ministry, he was told by Paul in 2 Timothy 4:2, "Be prepared in season and out of season." The concept of preparing is not a new one. So why is it that when we find ourselves in the middle seasons of our lives, we seem to be caught off guard when that sudden change comes? Or when the circumstances turn from helpful to harmful, or the challenge arises from seemingly nowhere? It seems we spend more time reacting than responding. These two words may seem similar in meaning, but they spring from a different starting point. *Reactionary living* is when you are playing catch-up to the changing situations around you. *Responsive living* is when you have grown an ability to choose a response that is immune from the situation's pressure points.

Responsive people are responsible people; they are not swayed by the crowd or by the circumstance. They have prepared their hearts and steadied their resolve. Reactionary living is like a roller coaster with twists and turns that you never expect. Responsive living anticipates the twists and has engaged a seat belt for the loop-the-loops. If in

> IT'S NEVER GOOD TO **GO TO THE MIDDLE AND FIND YOU'VE** PACKED ONLY ENOUGH GRACE FOR THE SHORE.

the middle you find your faith fails, your patience runs out, and you lose your peace, then you've likely not packed well for the journey. It's a bit like going all the way to the airport and finding out you've forgotten your passport. It's never good to go to the middle and find you've packed only enough grace for the shore. Paul knew there would be times when Timothy would be caught off guard—times when the ministry would take an unexpected turn, times when it would feel like spring, and times when he would need to be ready for the cold of winter. Timothy's level of preparedness was going to arm him with the ability to respond rather than react. I have found that the responders more often than not outlast the reactors. If we can respond well in the middle, then we can arrive intact at the end. Our willingness to pack well now, when it's calm, will ensure we endure well later in the storm.

If as the church we are called to help the world around us, then we have to learn how to do better in our responses. I wonder if the church has packed enough love, grace, wisdom, peace, and prayer today for the places they may end up tomorrow. If the church can't help the world "in season and out," who will? When we hear of injustice, have we already packed a response to bring justice? When the world faces trials, have we prepacked testimonies that have the power to overcome? We are called to be first responders to the world's needs, so we'd better start checking our bags and making sure we are packing well.

IN THE BAG

A few weeks ago, I was waiting to catch a train to our Leeds church campus. It was a quiet Sunday morning, with not many commuters waiting for the train. As I sat waiting on the bench, a gentleman pushing his bicycle arrived on the station platform and sat down next to me. It soon became apparent that he had injured himself. His cycling gear was all torn, and underneath the ripped material I could see a large, open wound that had a steady flow of blood coming from it. At closer inspection, he also had an injured hand and elbow, plus his bike looked a little bent out of shape. There was no one else there, so I inquired to see if I could somehow help. I was his first responder. He explained how a car, that had subsequently driven away, had just hit him, and he couldn't ride his bike as a result. He had hobbled to the train station so he could get home. He was clearly shaken up. I began to rummage through my rather large handbag, which my husband affectionately calls "the black hole," and within moments my bag went from an ordinary handbag to a temporary medical kit.

In my bag I found hand sanitizer and some wet wipes, with which I was able to clean and sterilize the cyclist's wounds. I also found Band-Aids. He didn't seem to mind that they had superheroes on them. Then, I found some sweets to give him a bit of sugar, as he seemed rather weak. Finally, I found water and some money for his train fare that he wasn't expecting to have to pay that day. My bag was packed with things that this situation required, so that in the first five minutes of meeting him at the train station I was able to take care of the worst of his complaints. Quite often, we face moments in life when we feel like this cyclist—knocked off our feet, bruised, and wounded—and we lack the supplies we need to survive because we never packed our bags correctly.

DESERT DRAMA

The children of Israel failed to find a positive first response to God's promise of deliverance from Egypt, and then went on to fail to respond well once they were set free. The journey to the promised land should have taken only days, but due to their poor response, this middle moment became a middle marathon. So what lessons can we learn from their desert drama? If they can turn a forty-day journey into a forty-year drama, then we are also susceptible to the same scenario.

When Moses went to tell the children of Israel that God was going to deliver them, they couldn't even listen to what God was saying because they were so disappointed.

> Moses reported this to the Israelites, but they did not listen to him because of their discouragement and harsh labor. (Exodus 6:9)

Their first response to Moses' good news was to allow their circumstances to control their confession. God was inviting them to freedom, but their response was disbelief. The enemy would love to create just enough discouragement in your soul so you are unable to respond to the opportunities that have the potential to move you forward. He wants you to be so aware of the demands of the current situation that you have no space to hear the call of the next invitation. The story of the children of Israel is such a tragedy—so much promise, provision, and purpose that all hinged on their response.

MIDDLE MOANERS

The children of Israel were moaners; they had a default moaning mode in their internal programming. We all have a "go-to setting." If you weren't sure what it was before the middle of a journey, it would soon reveal itself when you got there. Some people are always positive responders, others always negative. The children of Israel were professional moaners. They moaned about everything and anything. Not only did this almost drive Moses mad, but it eventually angered God.

As a parent, one of the most annoying moods to manage is that of a moaning child. The sound of the whining is enough to drive anyone crazy, but it is what's implicit within that moaning that is most bothersome. It suggests, "I am not happy and you should fix it." It says, "Entertain me and pander to me." It insists, "I am not willing to change this, but I am able to complain about this." Moaning in any child is annoying and unbecoming. God feels the same about that character trait in His children.

We have used several techniques for discipline as our children have grown up. One of the techniques we used when they were younger was the naughty step. The punishment of having to stay put on a step in the middle of a home full of activity would often prove to be an effective one. However, it took awhile for my son to learn that his response on the naughty step would either speed up his time spent there or extend it. I remember on one such occasion placing Noah on the naughty step for an argument he had had

> OUR STUBBORNNESS OR REBELLIOUS NATURE CAN **KEEP US STUCK ON A STEP** WE WERE ONLY MEANT TO **STOP ON TEMPORARILY.**

with his sister. While he sat there, he began to shout and plead his innocence. When he got no response, he began to shout all the louder at what he considered an injustice. Eventually he went quiet. Two minutes later, when we went to check on him, he had clearly given up and subsequently fallen asleep.

After waking him up, I explained his time on the step was

due to his response. At any time, he could have offered an apology to his sister or changed his attitude, and he would have found he was able to get off the step and join the activity around him. His stubbornness and defiance had led to this destination—sleeping in the middle of the hallway staircase. With God, our response works much the same. Our stubbornness or rebellious nature can keep us stuck on a step we were only meant to stop on temporarily. Noah soon learned how to manage the naughty step. He knew if he could find a sorry "quicker"—he could move on "faster." Eventually, he learned that if he would respond better to his sister in the first place, he could avoid the time-out altogether.

Where does your response need some work? What is your first response mode? Are you too fearful to say yes? Is your first response determined by the last bad situation you were in? Is it shaped by doubts, disappointments, or mistrust? Is your response cynical, critical, negative, or prideful? Do you need to learn how to become a better-equipped first responder? What if your first response to the things God brings to your life was love? What if you first responded with grace? What about a first response of praise? All these responses move us more quickly through our middles to the promise.

RESET

Awhile ago, I felt God challenge my own heart with this. I was in my hotel room in the U.S., getting ready for an event, and I felt God ask me to get on my knees and spend some time in His presence. After several hours of waiting on God, I simply felt Him nudge my response button. Where I had let weariness slip my response from yes to maybe, I knew God was asking me to reset and move to a yes response again. I had allowed the busy season of life to change my first response to a negative or resistant answer. No sooner had I reset my heart when I walked into a huge opportunity that I did not even see coming. When asked a question by the people I was meeting with, the first response I was armed with was a yes—which before my face time with God I know would have been a resounding no. It's good from time to time to check your responses as they have the power to change your future.

Moses led the children of Israel from a life of captivity and bondage to the promised land. But before they could possess the promise, they had to navigate the middle. The middle was where God wanted to confront their moaning and develop their trust. God had removed their physical chains of slavery, but the desert was all about creating a middle moment where they removed their internal bondage. It was where they needed to change their mind-sets from prisoner to possessor, from slave to child of God. The middle should have been their greatest season of growth and discovery, but because of their response it became a season of frustration and failure. The Israelites definitely needed some attitude adjustments, but rather than work with God, they decided instead to resist God.

DATA UPDATE

Awhile ago we changed our television set. Everything that plugged into it was the same, but when we installed the new set we did not update the settings. Therefore, we would often get to the middle of a movie and an error message would appear, informing us that we did not have sufficient data to continue. As I am not at all technically gifted, my response was to turn the TV off and give up, rather than try to proceed with what I was watching. But I realized when this happened to my kids, they were not so easily dissuaded. They were of the belief that this was their movie and they were going to watch it to the end. So they began to press buttons and enter codes, and before long, they had reset the screen so their movie could continue.

That's how it is on our journeys with God, when He is leading us from where we are to where we are to be next. Along the journey we may encounter a data error. For instance, data errors are common in a new place where we haven't yet updated the settings. In that scenario, we need to respond like my kids did—refuse to be daunted or intimidated into quitting, take control of the remote, and reset the screens. The children of Israel needed to reset their screens. They brought too much of the past into their middle. They needed to update the settings so that they could continue.

When I was frustrated with the TV set, I would ask my husband, "Why did we have to get this new one when the old one was just as good?!" Then he would remind me that the old TV was smaller, had a poor quality picture, didn't have great sound, and was old technology. But in my frustration, I had forgotten all of that. All I remembered was that it never gave me an error message. In the middle, we will either fight to move forward or romanticize the past. My memory of our old TV set was not accurate. In the middle of your transition, stepping up or changing, be careful of how you talk about and view your past.

POSTCARDS FROM THE PAST

Three days into their journey, the children of Israel became very aware of their hunger. Just three days after the Red Sea had opened and they had watched their enemies be destroyed, just three days after they had plundered their prisoners and they had moved from slave to free. Their response was challenged as they began to complain about the lack of food. They had gone back to their default mode of moaning. Exodus 16 explains:

> In the desert the whole community grumbled against Moses and Aaron. The Israelites said to them, "If only we had died by the Lord's hand in Egypt! There we sat around pots of meat and ate all the food we wanted, but you have brought us out into this desert to starve this entire assembly to death." (vv. 2–3)

The children of Israel began to romanticize the pots of meat they used to eat in Egypt; they became obsessed with their immediate hunger and lost sight of their long-term provision. Rather than focus on the free-flowing milk and honey on the horizon, they hungered for the stew they ate in slavery.

The enemy loves to send you postcards from your past. He will only select the parts he feels can get your interest, and he will choose his moments to post them to you. He sends you a card in your dark moments, saying, "Wish you were back here." He sent the Israelites a postcard of meat and edited out the pictures of the misery of their lifestyle. That's why we have to reprogram our memory in the middle. We need to pull our mind into line with our promise. If you open the post from the past in the middle, you will always have an inappropriate response.

WHAT IS IT?

God in His grace supernaturally provided an answer to the Israelites' hunger. But this food was not going to look like the food of Egypt. This food would be a miracle designed to sustain them in the middle. It would cause them to reprogram and change their appetite. This was food the Israelites had never seen before. In the middle, God will often satisfy our hunger in a way we have never seen before. He will answer in a way we did not expect, and He will take us into a season where we go back to school about how great our Creator God is.

This food supply was so unusual that they named it *manna*, which literally means, "What is it?" It was sent to not only feed the Israelites, but also to reprogram them. Don't be surprised if you receive some "What is it?" moments in the middle. Remember the disciples, when they saw Jesus on the water they also asked, "What is it?" They thought they were seeing a ghost. When Moses saw the burning bush speaking to him in the middle of his wilderness experience, he too asked, "What is it?" In the middle, God will provide meat for a prophet in the mouth of a meat-eating raven, He will send a whale to redirect a wayward prophet, and He will use a donkey to deliver a message and cause a wall to come down with a shout. The middle is where God's "What is it?" becomes your miracle.

IN THE MIDDLE, GOD WILL OFTEN SATISFY OUR HUNGER IN A WAY WE HAVE NEVER SEEN BEFORE.

Have you ever tried to introduce a new food into your diet, or cut out an old food that you knew was not good for you?

Awhile ago, I decided to get radical and start a new juice regime as part of my lifestyle. At first I found it quite overwhelming! I had to buy a juicer and then get all of the right vegetables. It was also time-consuming. At many points in my dietary changeover I was tempted to just give up. I even found a place online that could do it all for me and send me the juices ready-made. But the expense of that service was so high I persevered with my juicer.

It wasn't long before my new juice addition was having a visible benefit. I was feeling more energized and my system felt cleansed by the goodness of all the nutrients. The juicing changed my kitchen, my groceries, my choices, and my health. It was better for me, but it required a whole new discipline. The middle is where God will challenge those eating habits that are not good for us. He wants your diet to be closer to the food that He has for you in the promised land than the food you ate in slavery. Therefore, just as I had to learn how to juice, the children of Israel were going to have to learn how to do the manna diet.

The instructions for the collection of manna were simple; first they were to collect according to what they needed:

> This is what the LORD has commanded: "Everyone is to gather as much as they need. Take an omer for each person you have in your tent." The Israelites did as they were told; some gathered much, some little. And when they measured it by the omer, the one who gathered much did not have too much, and the one who gathered little did not have too little. Everyone had gathered just as much as they needed. (Exodus 16:16–18)

In Egypt they ate what they were given, but in the middle God wanted them to take what they needed. They were sent out and told to bring home their own supply according to their needs. Some gathered much and others little, but each ended up with exactly what was needed. I love that the Bible gives us this amount of description of how the manna miracle unfolded. There is a discipline in the middle of learning to take what you need.

Everyone has to respond for him or herself; we are to each go and take from God what we need. It's sometimes only in that desert experience that I have realized just how much I need. I have found in the middle my need for grace and for peace, and I have had to go and bring that into my life. In Egypt the Israelites ate what they were given, but in the desert they ate according to what they were willing to collect. Going back to my juicing regime, when I went for the prepackaged juices on a few occasions, I was never sure just how many vegetables they had blended to make my drink. I didn't know if they had added sugars or diluted the flavors. I just drank what I was given. But when I made my own juice, I took the produce I knew I needed and I added it to my juice.

The children of Israel were learning to go to the source for themselves; they were learning to bring in what they needed instead of being reliant on their captors to feed them. If you are in the middle, maybe you need to change the way you get fed. Stop going to the friend who always tells you what to do, stop listening to everyone else's revelations, don't always eat the advice somebody gives you, and let God be your source—go to Him to collect what you need. If you need wisdom, He has that. If you need peace, He has that. If you need healing, He has that! The miracle of manna was not just the provision but also the process. They were resetting their response from being slave-fed to being source-fed. We need to do the same. Don't romanticize the processed food of the past; embrace the miracle of manna in the middle.

MAGGOTS

The second instruction for the Israelites is in Exodus 16:19:

> Then Moses said to them, "No one is to keep any of it until morning."

This food supply was to be a daily discipline. They had to get up each morning and go get the fresh manna. However, many of the Israelites tried to save their supply for the next day, and when they went to check on the food the next morning, it was full of maggots! Moses was angry at their inability to follow God's directions so he rebuked the children of Israel. Whether they had saved the manna because they did not trust there would be enough in the morning, or they saved some as they were too lazy to collect it each morning, whichever the reasoning behind their rebellion—the end result was the same: what they tried to hold onto became rotten.

Rotten food is not pleasant in any instance, and food with maggots in it is even worse. God allowed what the Israelites held onto to become infested with termites so that there was absolutely no chance to reuse it. In the middle, we too can get a bad case of the maggots when we try to hold onto something God wants us to let go of. Old mind-sets, old habits, and wrong attachments all have to be addressed in the middle. Otherwise, they will rot your future.

Have you ever tried to save something for later? Not sure why you may need it, or if you will even want it, but you would rather know you have it than let it go. Before you know it, you have a house that is filled with "save it for later" items that are neither usual nor necessary. They take up valuable space, clutter your creativity, and shrink your space.

NEW DIET

When you enter a middle season of the journey, between where you have been and where you are going, it is always best practice to remove the maggots. Don't harbor anything rotten. Do an inventory of things that have passed their sell-by date and get rid of them. God didn't want the children of Israel to take rotting food into the promised land; He didn't want maggots in the place flowing with milk and honey. The only way to ensure that the new opportunity was not soured by the ways of slavery was to teach them to eat from a different source and to create disciplines that would mean their past could not contaminate their future.

Manna was a daily miracle; it was heaven-sent food. Yet the miracle in the middle soon became the very thing they would moan about the most. Instead of their response to the manna being one of amazement and wonder, and rather than being grateful for a God that not only delivered them but provided for them, the Israelites began to complain. They didn't see manna as the miracle it was. Instead, all they could think about was the meat that it wasn't. They began to think and talk about nothing more than the meat of Egypt, and the more they thought about it the more they fixated on it, and the more they craved it. Like a pregnant woman who decides there is only one food that can fulfill her needs, they became agitated and very vocal about how they wanted Moses to satisfy their cravings.

Moses, overwhelmed by their complaint, sought God and asked that the burden of these moaning people be removed. However, God was about to give them what they wanted, and in doing so, many of them would die for their choice of dinner over God's choice of diet. In the middle, be aware of what you crave. Cravings are very powerful—they will lie to you, they will over-promise and under-deliver. Cravings appeal to your senses and your flesh, whereas the things of God will speak to your spirit. The Israelites allowed their cravings to overwhelm them, and by doing so, they never made it to the promised land.

> But while they were still chewing the quail and had hardly swallowed the first bites, GOD's anger blazed out against the people. He hit them with a terrible plague. They ended up calling the place Kibroth Hattaavah (Graves-of-the-Craving). There they buried the people who craved meat. (Numbers 11:33–34 THE MESSAGE)

KIBROTH HATTAAVAH

God heard the moaning of the Israelites, the whining for the meat of Egypt, so He replied to their response. He sent so much quail meat into the desert that they were surrounded by the thing they had craved. As they began to eat the meat God sent a plague, and in that place many died. Their craving became their undoing; they named that place Kibroth Hattaavah, which means the "Graves of Craving." They had a promised land ahead of them, but they died with the meat of their past in their mouths. We must not allow the middle to choose our menu.

The best food source in the middle is not the one you request, but the source that God sends. It's the source that helps change your diet

DON'T LET WHAT YOU CRAVE PUT YOUR DESTINY IN THE GRAVE.

for your new destination. It's the provision that you go and gather. It's the fresh supply that has nothing rotten in it.

In the middle, you will find out sooner or later how strong your cravings are. Do you crave comfort more than courage? Do you crave the past more than the future? Is there a bigger craving in you for what you know than what you don't know? Do you crave control more than freedom? The children of Israel's craving for meat of the past starved them of their future. Don't let what you crave put your destiny in the grave. If you crave approval more than obedience, you will die in a grave built by your cravings. If you crave comfort more than calling, comfort will build you a resting place. The enemy is happy to fulfill your craving if he knows what you crave—for it will end up being your grave.

ACTION POINTS

1. What is your first response mode?
2. What new mind-set does your middle require?
3. What craving do you need to change?

PRAYER POINTS

1. Pray for strength to let go of the past.
2. Repent of the places your moaning has caused you to overlook God's miracle.
3. Pray with faith for your future and determination to reach your destination.

NINE

COMMUNAL CHANGE

I DON'T KNOW WHO SUGGESTED IT, OR WHY THEY THOUGHT it would be a good idea, but awhile ago I was talked into joining a gym. I was skeptical about whether it was possible for this to be a happy union as I am not a fan of Lycra, and I was stressed at just the thought of trying to figure out how to use the various kinds of complex gym apparatus. However, convinced I needed to change up my exercise routine, and with my kids continually asking that we find a place to go and swim, I began to look for a suitable gym to join. I had determined I was not going to allow myself to be easily converted by the gym fanatics. I also had a long list of requirements before I would consider handing over my membership fee.

In my search I visited several gyms, some of which were quickly dismissed from the list. At one gym, I didn't even make it past the front door, due to the overwhelming sweat odor that greeted me upon arrival. While at another gym, there were way too many Lycra-wearing enthusiasts for me to ever fit in.

Eventually, I settled on a gym that was not far from where I lived. It was located in a beautiful setting and it appeared to have what I would call "coffee culture" clientele. In other words, people went more for the Jacuzzi and lunch options than the weights and aerobic classes. So I bought all the gym gear and set off for my first official date as a new member! When I pulled up in the parking lot, I followed the procession of people to the entrance area. I chatted with a few regular members kind enough to show me the coffee shop and the way around. After a strong latte, I decided it was time to get started with a swim. I headed down the hall to a door that said Changing Rooms and as I walked through the door, little did I know everything I had thought about my nice new gym was about to change.

GOD HAS DESIGNED THIS JOURNEY SO THAT **WE HAVE TO LEARN HOW** TO CHANGE TOGETHER.

As the door opened into the female locker room, I had expected to see a well-equipped space with plenty of changing cubicles and lockers for each member. What I was not expecting was to be greeted by a huge communal changing area where right in front of my eyes women were in various states of undress. After the initial shock, I found myself trying to avoid eye contact with some of the same women who I had met earlier in the coffee shop, once again saying "hello," but this time with barely any clothes on. I was embarrassed for them, and sorry that I had walked in as they were trying to get changed—though they did not seem to share my embarrassment. I decided straightaway that this was not going to be the gym for me. I mean, where were the private cubicles? Why was everyone acting like this was normal? And then, as if I needed further confirmation that now was the time to leave, I heard someone say, "Hey, Pastor Charlotte, I didn't know you came here." No, this was definitely not for me.

EXPOSED

I have found that the middle makes me feel much the same as the gym did that day . . . exposed. The middle moments of our lives are typically where God seems to allow—and even expect—us to communally change. The times we would like to hide the most, can be the times when we seem to be seen the most. The things we wanted to go through on our own, seem to be witnessed by so many more people than we may deem necessary. The middle is where people will see your faith unwrapped and your fear exposed, where the doubts will be revealed and the layers of excuses are peeled away. The middle is where anything fake will be shaken and anything hidden will be seen, which is often why many people quit in the middle—deciding it is too embarrassing to change with so many people around to see them go through the process. However, God has designed this journey so that we have to learn how to change together.

Just think for a moment about the disciples. They were called to be on Jesus' team. He was going to change them from fishermen to fishers of men. He was going to challenge them to change from boys to men. He was going to take them from being dressed in doubts to wearing their beliefs out loud. This transformation for each of the disciples was going to happen over a short and intense period of time, and for the most part that change would not just be seen by the rest of the disciples but often by those they were meant to be leading. Though his intention was not to embarrass or expose them, Jesus did not hide the fact that the disciples were works in progress. He knew he didn't have time for them to be slow changers. If they were too proud to change in front of one another, they were not going to be able to get to where He needed them to be.

LEARNING ON THE JOB

In Mark 9, we read a catalog of changes that took place as Jesus rebuked, corrected, challenged, and asked the disciples to change, not only in front of each other but in front of the crowds that had gathered that day. And being Jesus' closest friends meant they needed to be willing to change quickly. In that same chapter, Jesus challenges Peter for wanting to camp in the place they were called to move on from. Then, He has to rebuke His disciples for unbelief as they fail to free a child from the torment of an evil spirit. Jesus not only shows them how it is done, but He speaks to their lack of faith—all in front of the watching crowd. Then He overhears the prideful conversation of the disciples who are asking who will be the greatest among them. Jesus doesn't ignore the comments, but instead exposes them and addresses their pride. He then goes on to challenge John's judgmental attitude toward those who are using Jesus' name, and his refusal to accept them as they are not yet one of their group. Jesus corrects John's decision in front of the others and challenges his perspective about those they are actually called to work with.

Though each encounter happens in quick succession, without long explanations or carefully planned timing, so as to minimize hurting the disciples' feelings, Jesus seems immune to feeling the need to be oversensitive or cautious in how He corrects His team. He doesn't create a private individual change area. More often than not He dealt with the disciples publicly. He also dealt with mistakes quickly as He expected the disciples to change rapidly and move on. He knew if they couldn't remain with Him while He was pruning them, then they would lose momentum and never be able to make the journey He had destined for them to take.

Jesus only had three years to help these boys change, so the communal changing room became the streets where they preached, on the grass where He fed people, and in the places where he healed and delivered those who were bound. Jesus needed a willingness from them to keep changing and courage to do it communally. I am sure Peter didn't want anyone to know about his imminent denial. In fact, when Jesus told him what was ahead he refused to accept this would be something he would do. But Peter had to go through the communal changing room. Not only did the disciples see Peter fail, but we are still preaching today from his denial moment. Jesus did not hide the process Peter went through. Instead, He took him through the changing room and clothed him with a new identity. He affirmed him and changed what would be detrimental to his future. The denial was an exposing moment, but because Peter stayed in the changing room it also became a defining moment.

God's intention is not to embarrass us but to help us understand that unless we are willing to change, we will never be able to go to the next place. No one enters a changing room with the intention of staying in the same clothes. The whole reason you go in is so you can put something else on that will be more appropriate for where you are going next. That day at the gym, I went in the changing room because I wanted to swim, but if I went swimming in the clothes I had on I would struggle and possibly sink. I needed a place that was in between the two to change attire.

REMAIN OR RUN

> I am the true vine, and my Father is the gardener. He cuts off every branch in me that bears no fruit, while every branch that does bear fruit he prunes so that it will be even more fruitful . . . Remain in me, as I also remain in you. (John 15:1–2; 4)

John 15 tells us that we are going to be pruned. Note the word "all"—that means nobody, not even the most flourishing person, is immune from pruning, from being changed. Why? Because God made change essential for your growth! But the verse goes on to say that when we are pruned we have to remain in the vine; we have to stay attached to God and to His body. Therefore, our changes are to happen in front of all the other branches. So often we want to detach to become pruned; we want to run away on our own and then face the problem; we want to escape a public crisis. God's choice is that we stay attached and let Him prune us in the communal changing place called the vine.

The truth is, we are usually in one of two camps; we either

choose to remain or have an urgency to run. Remaining is not always easy. There are times when running can seem far more attractive. In Genesis 16, we find the story of Hagar who found herself in the middle of a situation that caused her to run. Hagar was the maidservant of Sarah, Abraham's wife. After many years of Abraham and Sarah remaining childless, they

IN EVERY MIDDLE MOMENT, BE CAREFUL OF THE MOTIVATION BEHIND YOUR MOVEMENTS.

decided to try to move through their middle faster by manufacturing their own miracle. They couldn't wait for the promised child; instead, they would provide God some assistance and use Hagar to conceive the child that God had said they needed to trust Him for. Abraham and Sarah's impatience produced an awkward and unwanted situation for Hagar, who unexpectedly found herself in the middle.

When Hagar became pregnant with the boy Ishmael, her ability to stay where she had been settled for so long became extremely difficult. Hagar's place in the household of Abraham and Sarah suddenly changed, as her pregnancy became a source of great hostility in the home. Where she had previously been considered family, now she was an unwanted guest and a constant reminder of the mistake impatience had birthed.

On our journey through life, there will be seasons we have to face, as Hagar did, when we feel misunderstood, even mistreated, when the circumstances around us cause us to want to run away. And though there are times when separation can be part of God's strategy for our future, there are also times when fear will separate what God intended to stay together. Therefore, we need to discern the reasons why we choose to move on, especially when it is in a season where the pressure is on. If it is God-driven, then He will lead the way. But if our pain drives it, then be very careful. Hagar was now seeking to run away from the very place she had run to. She wanted to avoid the people she had come to call family. In every middle moment, be careful of the motivation behind your movements. Are you running away from where God wants and needs you to stay?

RELATIONAL RUNNER

One of the main reasons we choose to run and not remain can come down to relational dysfunction. So often in the middle, the relational messes we experience can turn "remainers" into "runners." While Sarah's mistreatment of Hagar was without excuse, Hagar had a home in this land. These people were her friends and family. She let the things that were being done to her threaten the future God had placed within her. Our remaining has to persevere through any similar relational test. Otherwise, we will never be in one place for very long.

When we choose to remain, we have to find the courage to stand our ground so we don't lose ground. I have experienced times in my journey when the relational breakdown around me has made me want to run. I remember in one instance being so hurt by someone who I thought had my back, only to find out that they actually had stuck a knife in it. I knew staying in the place where I felt the most pain would be hard, but I also knew running would worsen the wound. To remain relationally is a lesson we all have to learn. Jesus remained with the disciples through betrayal and doubts. He remained with those He was sent to save, even when those same people said "crucify Him." Our remaining must be in God first. So unless God asks us to move, we need to know how to stay put.

If there is a place in your world where intimidation is setting the direction, you need to go back and fix your coordinates. Our true-north direction needs to come from God and His Word for our life. So much of the growth we could have had is lost because of the people we feared, or the opinions we allowed to redirect us. God did not tell Hagar to go; He wanted her to stay. Sarah used her position to make Hagar's life impossible. But it's at those points where we feel the pressure from people that we need to remain in His presence.

Don't allow the enemy to use relationships to make you run. There will always be a Sarah, a Goliath, or a Saul. But just because they may appear in our middle, we don't have to let them determine our ending! Learn how to remain relationally. Let God be the One you are rooted in. Let your relationship with Him decide how you respond to the other relationships you encounter. Too much time is lost when we fail to remain and go on the run. Challenge is inevitable and change is necessary, but God's plan is that you change while you remain.

RESPONSIBILITY RUNNER

Hagar now had a responsibility named Ishmael. This baby was growing inside of her; she was responsible not just for her remaining but also for his. He was attached to whatever she attached to, and if she disconnected, so did he. So often in the times when we have an urgency to run, we forget what is within us. We forget that our remaining is not just about ourselves, but it's about all those others God has for us to help and reach.

Responsibility is a word that some love and others want to avoid. If I mention the word "chores" in earshot of my children they will run for the hills, as they know that "chores" means it's time for them to take care of what we have deemed their responsibility. It's amazing how at chore time they suddenly want to call a friend, remember they have homework, or want to read the book they have never picked up. They will look for any distraction to avoid taking care of their responsibilities.

> **GOD RARELY UPROOTS OUR LIVES. HE IS A GREAT BELIEVER IN THE POWER OF PLANTING.**

We can be the same when it comes to our own destiny in God. We have things He wants to give us as our responsibility—callings and gifts. However, if we don't mature in the middle, we—like my children—will think of many other things we would rather do than the thing that God is asking us to do. We want to run to something that seems less demanding and escape changing in a way that we know will be costly. That's why God wants us to remain, because remaining in the middle means accepting our responsibility.

When I was twenty years of age, I went to a conference in America where for the first time I heard a female preach the Word of God. As soon as I saw the way this woman communicated comfortably in her own skin, I was able to visualize what God had been calling me to do. The problem was I didn't know how that would fit inside our church. At the time, there were no female speakers. They had no room for that kind of ministry, and yet, I now felt I had this responsibility growing on the inside of me. My first reaction was like Hagar's, to run. I didn't want to be responsible for what I was feeling and seeing. I wanted to sidestep the task I felt God was asking me to carry out. I didn't want people to see me changing and growing in this way.

Jonah tried to run from his responsibility and God sent him back in a whale. Moses tried to run from his responsibility and God redirected him with a burning bush. Elijah tried to run away from Jezebel and God sent him back to anoint his successor. Remaining is not easy, but we can't allow the fear of the responsibility to dislodge our destiny.

Hagar was frightened of the reactions people around her would have. She was intimidated and scared, and so to avoid any confrontation and to try to skip the changing process, she became a girl on the run. In verse 9, as she sits by the side of the road, she hears God's voice. The direction He gives her is: *"Hagar, go home."* His plan for Hagar was not for her to be a spiritual hobo, roaming around from place to place.

Change doesn't necessarily mean everything has to change. When the leaves on trees change color in the fall months, the process does not uproot the tree. Changes are happening within the leaves themselves, and on the branches, but the tree remains planted. The same is true for us. When change happens in the middle, while some things may vary in color, or even fall away, we're not uprooted. God rarely uproots our lives. He is a Great Believer in the power of planting.

In the middle, it's important to discern the differences between running and remaining. Too many people run from the pressure, the pain, or the challenge, but what if more of us remained? What would that look like? Though the change may feel uncomfortable, and at times embarrassing, don't allow those temporary moments to make permanent decisions. Let's not allow moments of discomfort to divide what God is able to unite.

CHANGING RULES

That day at the gym I had to decide: Did I want to go swimming or go home? Did I want to stay unhealthy or get fit? Was I going to remain a member of this club or was I going to run for the exit? If this gym membership was going to be any use at all, I was going to have to not just show up once a year, but at least once a week if not more! I finally faced the more important question: Was my level of embarrassment going to determine my commitment? It took a little personal pep talk before I decided to get changed, but once I was in the pool, I realized just how pathetic I had been.

If you, like me, have an aversion to changing rooms, consider these communal changing room rules that will help you remain in the vine while your life is being pruned.

RULE ONE: DON'T STARE

Whenever I took the kids to the gym for their swimming lessons, or to burn off some energy for a few hours, we'd enter through the double doors of the changing room and I would say to them, "When we get in there, remember not to stare." They would assure me they wouldn't . . . but as any inquisitive five year old would tell you, that was extremely difficult!

In our middle moments we need a "no staring" understanding. If we can all accept that this is where many of us will be challenged to change, where our ugly parts may be exposed, and what we had hidden for so long will be revealed, then we need to extend to one another the "no stare" policy. Frankly, people who stare in any situation are slightly creepy, but those who would stare at you in your most vulnerable moments—well, I would say they are just weird.

Staring makes the person who is already embarrassed even more self-conscious. We need to allow one another some space in the middle. Staring can look like asking questions that make you feel more awkward than you already do. Staring is the overemphasis on the problem and the undervaluing of the answer. Staring highlights what's wrong rather than helps put things right. We can stare

> WE NEED TO ALLOW **ONE ANOTHER SOME** SPACE IN THE MIDDLE.

with our words, with our actions, with our tweets, and our comments. Staring was what the people did to the woman who was caught in adultery. They dragged her into the market square and drew attention to her failure, then stared at her sin until Jesus came and told them to start looking at themselves before they stared too long at the sin in another.

Staring makes the middle so much more miserable when you know where you are deficient. You don't need others to keep reminding you. If someone in your world is going through the middle of a marriage struggle, don't stare, don't embarrass him or her, and don't point a finger or judge. Let's have a no-stare policy for the teenager struggling to change their attitude and behavior. Instead of exposing them and exaggerating their mess, let's focus on their future and what God says about them. Staring churches scare people away, staring parents make children never feel good enough, and staring friends strain relationships. Staring makes remaining more difficult, and we need each person to stay connected if they are going to make it. So the less we stare, the more people can stay the course in the middle.

RULE TWO: PROVIDE COVER

Have you ever been to the ocean and wanted to quickly change so you could go in the water? Instead of going back to the house or hotel to change, you decide to try to change on the beach. You ask someone you think you can trust to hold several towels around you to provide you with some cover. For those few moments, their towel holding becomes crucial to your ability to change. The same is true in the middle. In that place where we feel the need to change, we also need to be willing to provide cover. If staring exposes, then love covers. And in the communal change area, we need plenty of willing towel holders providing cover for one another. This does not mean we are hiding things that God needs to heal, but it does mean we are aiding the change rather than alienating people in the change.

Cover can look like praying, it can look like taking care of the things that are slowing the change process down, it can look like sowing seed or showing mercy. It may mean carrying the load so another can get help. In the changing room, if we all enter willing to provide cover then we make the middle a place where grace and mercy flow. Somehow, we have made getting counseling a sign of failure rather than something that helps provide cover. In the middle, we need more towels of grace, towels of love and mercy, and towels that help people get the change they need.

Over many years of serving in the local church, I have seen various examples of where the right cover has helped people remain, helped them find the strength to say "I'm sorry" to move into forgiveness, or to deal with their bitterness—all made possible because someone said "let me help you." I have seen single moms dealing with unforgiveness from their broken marriage receive help to change when someone has said, "let me help watch your children; let me give you some space to go and get help." I have seen families take wayward children into their home to give them some safe cover, while they deal with the things

IF STARING EXPOSES, THEN LOVE COVERS.

that are creating stress in their life. Cover is something we will all need at some point. The more of us that enter the changing room with a towel, the less we will feel the need to expose what God's grace wants to cover. We are not here to cover up the mistake, or bury the bad attitude. We are here to create an environment that moves hurt to a place of healing.

RULE THREE: NO PHOTOGRAPHS ALLOWED

Any public changing room will normally have a sign somewhere prohibiting photographs from being taken. I think in God's communal changing room we need to post the same signs!

Photographs capture a moment but they don't tell the whole story. Let's not lock people in a moment that God has meant for them to pass through.

Growing up in the same church all my life, I have come to realize how important this rule is. When I was a teenager, I had many middle moments when I was not pleasant to be around. I went through the annoying know-it-all stage. I had a rebellious heart, an obnoxious attitude, and had to learn to submit to authority. All of these changes took place in the same church, surrounded by many of the people I still do life with today— people who were my youth pastor, life group leader, and who taught me and disciplined me. But now as the pastor of that same church, those same people are allowing me to disciple and lead them. That is only possible because not one of them took a photograph in the middle. They haven't frozen me in time around one of the moments when I was failing and floundering. They don't pull out the photograph of my mistake to remind me of my inadequacy. Rather, they have let me go in and out of that changing room as many times as I have needed, and they have allowed me to grow with each change into who God wants me to be.

I have been around churches and leaders who have photograph albums full of pictures of people they have frozen in time. When you suggest a name of someone who could help or step up in an area, they are all too willing to pull the photograph out of where they last failed to remove them from the possible candidates that could be used in this opportunity. Stop taking pictures of each other that become like a collection of mug shots of middle moments. God doesn't take photographs. If He did, how would He be able to go and get the murderer Moses out of the middle of the desert to use him as a deliverer of millions of people? If God took mug shots, then He could have never used Saul, "the persecutor," to become the apostle Paul, or Peter "the denier" to build His church.

Many people are unable to leave the changing room because someone hung their photograph on the wall. It is a picture of them in their most exposed moment. Now no one can see past their failure or faltering that was freeze-framed for all time. We need to ban cameras from the middle. But from time to time, we also need to check our photo albums to see if we have frozen someone else in time.

SELFIES

As a note of caution in a world obsessed with "selfies": don't freeze yourself in time. Don't take a selfie in your mess, then punish yourself by obsessing on the mistake you made. Don't take a selfie of your scars and hurts. Be kind to yourself. Allow God to help you change well. Don't let the enemy use your state of undress to question your calling. Don't take the selfie that says "I'm a failure," "I doubted," "I questioned," "I betrayed," or "I denied Him."

Following Peter's three-time denial of Jesus in their first conversation after His resurrection, Jesus asks him the same question three times. "Peter, do you love Me?" With each affirming "yes" that Peter gave, Jesus helped him delete the seflie he had taken in his three denial moments. Jesus wasn't going to allow anyone to take a photograph of Peter "the denier" when He knew he was called to be Peter "the builder." This disciple may have gone through the communal change, but Jesus was going to make sure no photographs were posted that held Peter as a prisoner to his past. Peter needed to delete his own old photographs, but Jesus did it for him. He forgave Peter faster than Peter could forgive himself.

IN IT TOGETHER

The key to me finally changing at the gym—not just once but as many times as I desired to go and work out—was when I came to this realization: everyone was in the changing room for the same reason. There was something they wanted to do; a place they wanted to go that required them to change. We were just all in different stages of changing. Some had almost finished getting changed, others were just beginning, some had lots of layers to remove, while others came with half of their gym clothes already on. Yet everyone was there to change because they desired to move on to somewhere else.

Jesus said to remain on the vine "remain in me." Why? Because we are all getting pruned together—we will all see the good, the bad, and the ugly, the fruitful and the thorns. Each branch was going to be pruned to become stronger, healthy, and better. So if you are on the vine, just look around and realize God's designed it so we change alongside each other, so we can support one another and not feel isolated in the moments when we are most vulnerable.

Don't leave the gym because you are embarrassed to change. Instead, understand that by changing you'll get to move on to a different environment; you get to work out and become stronger; you get to dive into the pool and go deeper. Don't be robbed from what waits at the other side of the changing room doors, because we are all in this together.

ACTION POINTS

1. Identify the areas you need to change.
2. Deal with the places where running is hindering your remaining.
3. Determine to follow the communal changing rules.

PRAYER POINTS

1. Pray for the patience to change.
2. Pray for the strength to be planted so that you can flourish.
3. Pray for the grace to allow those around you to change alongside you.

TEN

AFTER THE GIANT

THE RHYTHMICAL CHANT OF "ARE WE THERE YET?" COMING from the backseat of the car—which had provided the soundtrack thus far on our journey—eventually turned into the question, "Where are we?" "Good question," was my reply. I only knew where we weren't. We weren't at the hotel where our nice comfortable bed and room service were prepared and waiting. And we weren't at home, as we had left hours earlier. After enduring several unforeseen traffic jams and detours, I also wondered where we were. Towns between the start and end destination were not something I had paid any attention to, since they were just places we would be passing through. But now that the children had asked the question, I took on the challenge of deciphering the map, to at least try to bring a little more clarity to our whereabouts.

Once we had established our location, it was not long before the next question came: "Is there somewhere we can stop? We're hungry." At this point, my husband agreed a food stop was a good idea, and we agreed to find a place to refuel and replenish the passengers and crew. I looked for somewhere close by that had all the necessary amenities. Preferably, we could make this a quick intermission—find a drive-through, gas station, and restroom all in the same vicinity.

We chose a place close to the main road we were traveling along, so that it wouldn't take too much of our time. I can't remember the name of the place where we refueled the car and ourselves that day. I only remember it served a purpose to satisfy our needs, allowing us to carry on to our chosen destination. As we drove away, we passed row upon row of neat little cottages that looked so inviting. I thought about how this place where we had barely stopped for thirty minutes was for others where they had chosen to live for possibly thirty years. For some, this was their beloved hometown, a place that held many fond memories. For us, it was merely where we had passed through. We had no interest in extending our time there, as the more time we spent, the less time we would get to spend in our prepaid weekend destination.

PASSING THROUGH

In life, we will come upon these kinds of scenarios many times over—times when we will need to come off the road, rest, and refuel. But we must never be tempted to make these temporary stopping places our permanent address. Weariness and a desire to be fed now can convince us to add an unscheduled stop on our trip. And while these stops are at times beneficial and necessary, we must never forget that the detour is not our final destination. Even if others are happily living where you are temporarily stopping, don't become confused. If this is not the place you had set out for, then it's not the place for you to unpack your life.

In Genesis 13, we read of the relationship between Abram and Lot. Abram loved his nephew Lot. After the death of his brother, Abram took on the responsibility for this now fatherless boy, raising him as his own. They worked the land and reared their cattle together. And God's smile was on Abram and all he did. However, the story of Abram and Lot does not end as well as it starts. Lot decided to make Sodom, a place they were passing, his permanent address. It was there that his journey filled with trouble, which eventually led to his demise.

Over the years, I have heard many lessons on Lot's failings. For instance, how he was a bad man who needed to separate from God's good man, Abram. Yet, 2 Peter 2:7 in Scripture records a somewhat different account. It says Lot was "a righteous man, who was distressed by the depraved conduct of the lawless." Lot, like many of us, was a person who was on a journey, and at some point he made a miscal-

IF THIS IS NOT THE PLACE YOU HAD SET OUT FOR, THEN IT'S NOT THE PLACE FOR YOU TO UNPACK YOUR LIFE.

culation, allowing his detour to change his destiny. The wrong choices in the middle can move us into the wrong neighborhoods. Like Lot, we can move from the alignment that Abram offers to an attachment that can torment our soul.

In Genesis 12, God made it very clear to Lot where he should attach and the direction he was to go in God. He promised:

The Lord had said to Abram, "Go from your country, your people and your father's household to the land I will show you. I will make you into a great nation, and I will bless you; I will make your name great, and you will be a blessing. I will bless those who bless you, and whoever curses you I will curse; and all peoples on earth will be blessed through you." (vv. 1–3)

There was a blessing on Lot if he remained aligned to Abram. So why would he leave the place of blessing for a place called Sodom? In the same way, why would we derail our own destinies with our own hands? Sadly, Lot's story is not an uncommon one. It could happen to any of us.

TOO MUCH STUFF

As much as we can associate the middle with the hard times and struggles, we can also enjoy great moments in the middle—moments where we can see God's providence and provision, where His favor strengthens us, and His kindness provides for us. These moments in our middle can bring a sense of comfort and satisfaction that can go on to convince us that we have journeyed far enough.

Our successes can cause us to stop just as much as the sorrows. Just as quickly as our trials can derail us, so can our triumphs. In fact, it's often in the times of increase we are most tempted to stop. We want to prolong the feeling that success affords us and stay in the bubble our contentment brings. No matter how great a time we are having in these moments, we eventually have to wrap up the party and move on.

God was blessing Abram and Lot in all they put their hands on. They were surrounded by increase and their blessing was so great it was beginning to slow them down. The crops and cattle they owned had become so vast it was hard to move forward together. So rather than lighten the loads, or find more space to expand, they separated. In verses 5–13 of Genesis 13, Lot decides he has accumulated so much stuff he is now content to settle. And he decides his possessions are more of a priority than his partnership with Abram. His accumulation of stuff causes the separation from his source, God, and he chooses to settle in Sodom.

I spend a lot of time traveling, so when it comes to luggage I am pretty good at knowing what my baggage allowance should be on any given flight. No matter how indecisive I may be feeling about which shoes I want to take, I know at some point I have to make a decision about what I am willing to leave behind, or there will be no room left to take the

OUR SUCCESSES CAN CAUSE US TO STOP JUST AS MUCH AS THE SORROWS.

things that I actually need. The middle is when you discover if you are over your baggage allowance and where God will ask you to lighten your load—to determine what is essential so you can focus on what is crucial for your future.

Lot had a lot! He was overrun with resources and riches to the point where he couldn't see *who* he had because of *what* he had. He confused his stuff and his source. God's plan was for Abram and Lot to stay together and for them to move forward together, but stuff got in the way. Sadly, I have seen this happen far too often—where God joins people for purpose but those same people become separated over something as insignificant as possessions, gifts, and abilities, or even ministry and callings becoming more important than their unity. "My way" becomes more important than "God's way." As a result, teams split and generations divide, all because we have a spatial issue that seems to be more important than our spiritual values. If we are not willing to lessen our baggage there's no way we'll arrive at our destinations together, with each generation helping the next.

PARTNERSHIP OR POSSESSIONS

We recently redecorated our son's bedroom. It was in need of an update. But, also, wanting to follow in his father's footsteps he had requested a drum kit for his birthday. In order to fit this kit into his room, we needed to clear some things out. One Saturday afternoon, we asked Noah to look through all his toys and books and decide what he still needed and what we could donate to another family. At first, the donate pile was rather sparse, while the keep pile was overflowing. That is until Noah remembered that the purpose of this clear out

> SOMETIMES IN THE **MIDDLE YOU HAVE TO** RE-EVALUATE WHAT **MATTERS MOST.**

was to give him a room that was more grown-up, a room that would have a drum kit in it. All of a sudden, his pile of keeps was reduced and his desire to donate was increased.

Routinely, we allow our stuff to keep us small. We want to keep hold of it all, but in doing so we retard our own growth. Lot had too much stuff. It was time for a clear out, time to make some decisions that would help them renavigate spatial problems. It was time to get some new land and a better system for managing their cattle. But rather than contain the problem so they could continue their progress, they allowed the issue to contaminate the camp.

Lot's herdsmen were now fighting with Abram's herdsmen. Because they failed to deal with the issue at the source, it became an issue in the ranks, and the virus of discontentment and disagreement spread to all those who were attached to these two leaders. Now brothers were turning against each other and the tension was creating division. Genesis 13 explains:

> So Abram said to Lot, "Let's not have any quarreling between you and me, or between your herders and mine, for we are close relatives. Is not the whole land before you? Let's part company. If you go to the left, I'll go to the right; if you go to the right, I'll go to the left." (vv. 8–9)

Abram appeals to Lot as a brother. He reminds him that their relationship is more important than their riches—and, still, the excess leads to Lot's exit. Lot would go on to discover that sometimes in the middle you have to re-evaluate what matters most. Are you more passionate about your possessions or your partnership? Are you more committed to your stuff than your source? Is the success of where you have come to stopping you from seeing any further?

What if Lot and Abram had stayed together? What if they had made different choices? Then Sodom, a place known for sin and selfishness, would have been less populated. There are times in the middle where, like my son Noah, you need to clear some space for the bigger purpose; you need to see that what you let go of is actually helping you attain something better. I have been through seasons in my life where I have wanted to camp out in my contentment. But on each of those occasions, I have realized that the decision to live in the neighborhood of Sodom has more to do with self than sacrifice, and the reason I want to stay has more to do with keeping my stuff than losing my life.

LET LOVE LEAD

We need relationships that pull us to the promise; we need conversations that place the cause above our convenience—that values doing things right more than being right. In the middle we need to not hang around the fighting herdsmen, but instead find the strategic shepherd who is more concerned with finding a resolve than his resources. Too many people drown in the middle, caught up in stuff that weighs them down. In the middle we allow relationships to die that God wanted us to journey through to the end. Abram loved Lot, and Lot loved Abram, but greed, not love, led in this middle moment.

When love leads you in the middle, you will find it easy to give some things up so that you can keep other things alive. When love leads, you will speak less about your stuff and more about your source. When love leads, you will see your brother, not your competitor. When love leads, you will unite in the struggle, not divide. Sometimes in the middle we need to ask ourselves who is leading? Have we let our needs, ambition, pride, and greed lead?

TREADING WATER

As I mentioned earlier, my son and daughter both took swimming lessons when they were younger. Getting from one end of the pool to the other was a lot of work for a four-year-old, so their instructor would always let them know that if they became overwhelmed in the water, or too weary to carry on, that they should tread water until she could come and pull them over to the side. I watched my children on many occasions use this technique to stop them from going under. They would stop swimming and start treading, so that there was just enough movement to keep them afloat until the teacher could take them over to the side where they could once again find their footing.

We need to learn to tread water in our grace, our patience, our speech, and our actions. We may be frustrated, we may even feel the desire to fight to be heard or proved right, but treading water is all about regaining control. It's just enough movement to keep you afloat until you can find the next stroke. It's finding a resolve without losing the relationship; it's saying enough, but not too much. Love knows how to **LOVE KNOWS HOW TO TREAD WATER IN A WAY THAT PRIDE DOESN'T.** tread water in a way that pride doesn't. Love treads through the situations offense would sink into. Love knows how to hold its head above the waves rather than drown in the pressure.

Lot became a resident of Sodom; he took his family, his staff, and possessions to a place that eventually would cost him everything. Instead of teaching his people to tread water, Lot took them to a place where they would eventually drown. I don't want to allow my impatience and frustration to damage the people I love. I want to be willing to tread water when I have to. Even if I don't like everything that's going on, I want enough tread in my trust that I keep afloat long enough to know that God is on His way to pull me over to the side.

When I reflect on my journey thus far, I am so aware of the people who have tread water for me to have the voice, the space, and the place I am now flourishing in. Their willingness to keep treading water stopped others and me from drowning. Abram went back to try to rescue Lot some time later in Genesis 14. His love for Lot had never changed, but the separation meant his ability to save him had been compromised.

PIT STOPS

I have been involved in many different types of work throughout my life. I've worked in a store, and then I managed a store. I've worked on my degree, in radio and television, in recruitment, and have managed a business. All of these jobs were on the way to something else—my end destination. I knew in my heart that God had spoken to me about being in ministry. I didn't fully understand what that looked like, but each stage in the journey—from one job to the next—was a temporary pit stop in my mind. It was a place to earn my wages, to pay my bills, to learn new skills, and to grow in my leadership ability. I worked hard, learned what I could, but also kept moving forward, trusting God, and at times treading a lot of water.

I remember in one season of my working life, the company I was employed by offered me a great promotion. Though this was an excellent move for my career, it came with a great cost. I would be required to relocate away from my family, my friends, and my church. Though the move looked impressive on paper, it was going to take me further away from what I knew in my heart God was calling me to do. In actuality, this move was not going to carry me closer to my future, but further away from it.

The art of managing the middle can be found in refusing the temptation to adapt permanent behavior in a temporary place. Any Formula One driver will tell you that pit stops are not destinations; they are refueling stations. They are not equipped for every eventuality; they are there to take care of the immediate need and emergencies. The middle of our journey is exactly the same: whether we end up there because we are out of fuel or because we need new tires, we are not there to stay.

Like a Formula One team, you need the right people at your pit stops. You need those who will refuel you, and not drain you. You need those who know how to get you back on the road and not try to get you out of the car. We need those who help us to keep going, not slow us down. Every person in that pit stop is watching the clock, knowing his or her purpose is to help his or her team member cross that finish line in the fastest time possible.

The relationships we forge in the middle will either propel us forward or hold us back. Therefore, more than any other time, we need to check our relational alignment at the places in our journey where we may make some unscheduled stops. Some of the best friendships I have ever discovered have been found in the middle. But, some of the biggest relational sabotages can be waiting in that very same space. Over these next few pages, take a relational inventory of your life—look for the refuelers, the ones who will help get you back on the road, and those who are trying to make your pit stop your last stop.

JUST CHEESE

David was destined to make a journey that would take him from the pasture to the palace, from a kid to a king, and from shepherding sheep to leading God's people. This journey would take David into many different pit-stop moments. And the relationships he needed for the journey were awaiting him in those places—but in the same space were relationships that would try to sabotage his success.

On one such day, David was running errands for his father. He took some cheese and bread to his brothers who were on the battlefield. While there, David heard a giant speaking blasphemy against his God. He could not ignore it, so instead of just moving on, David made a quick pit stop to take care of business. David's whole approach to Goliath tells you he was not intending to make this moment into something

THERE ARE MOMENTS WHEN OUR WILLINGNESS TO SERVE PLACES US ON THE FRONT LINE.

more permanent. First of all, David refused the offer to fight in the king's armor. A more prideful person would have been flattered at the opportunity to parade around in the king's shiny suit. But David did not want the added weight of the armor or the baggage it brought with it. David was more concerned about taking care of business than looking like the business. He refused the sword they handed him and, instead, took out the slingshot he had always used and aimed for the giant he couldn't miss. As soon as the giant fell, David finished the job and chopped off his head, after which he had every intention of getting back to his sheep.

But what happened after the giant holds important lessons for us all. Goliath became a big reveal moment for David. This unknown shepherd boy was now suddenly the people's champion. In those few moments, David went from zero to hero in the eyes of all those watching. The giant that had tormented them came tumbling down—all thanks to David.

This young boy, who had killed lions and bears with his own hands in private with no applause, was now being praised and idolized by the crowd for the one giant he killed in public. The unscheduled stop that day on his way to deliver some cheese was now becoming quite an event. The people began to cheer for David and sing songs about his quest; they wanted to turn this "rock slinger" into their "rock star." But amidst all of the accolades, David was aware of his own destiny and knew the giant was not supposed to define him. David was a shepherd, a worshipper, a man after God's own heart, but in these moments more people were drawn to the giant's head in his hands than were drawn to his heart for God.

In 1 Samuel 17, David was sent to see the king with Goliath's head still in his hands:

As soon as David returned from killing the Philistine, Abner took him and brought him before Saul, with David still holding the Philistine's head. (v. 57)

Be careful of the people who suddenly want to be on your team after your success. Saul had no interest in David until David had everybody's interest. Now Saul could see that this boy had the potential to further his own kingdom and boost his own prospects. Saul was not interested in David's heart; he was focused on what he could do with the giant's head in his hands.

In the middle are Goliath moments. They are the moments you did not look for, but they came and found you. Moments that God will create to take your life from hidden to seen, and to move you from obscurity into a place of opportunity. God was in charge of the timing of this giant; it was part of His plan to elevate David's profile. David, however, had to learn that this giant was not sent to define him, only to align him for the next season God had for his life.

We can all experience these Goliath-type moments in our middle. They are the times when the story of your fight becomes a platform for others to find faith. There are moments when our willingness to serve places us on the front line. These are the times when our "yes" to delivering cheese becomes God's "yes" to slaying giants. The thing about these moments is that you are as surprised as everyone else when they happen. They may not have been a part of your plan, but they are a part of God's. God uses middle moments to further His purpose.

BEHEADING AND BEFRIENDING

With the head fresh from the giant's neck still in his hands, David found himself summoned to a conversation with the king. Saul, after seeing David's success, wanted to be his friend.

The kid—who before wouldn't have been permitted in the same space as Saul—was now invited in for supper.

In times of acceleration, watch out for the people who may now suddenly request your company. Your Goliath moments will increase the places and people you may get to go and see, but be careful you aren't so impressed by Saul that you fail to see Jonathan. In the same room where Saul would seek to control David, God had positioned Jonathan, whom He had destined to serve David.

In 1 Samuel 18, Jonathan's reaction to David is very different from his father's response.

> After David had finished talking with Saul, Jonathan became one in spirit with David, and he loved him as himself. From that day Saul kept David with him and did not let him return home to his family. And Jonathan made a covenant with David because he loved him as himself. Jonathan took off the robe he was wearing and gave it to David, along with his tunic, and even his sword, his bow and his belt. (vv. 1–4)

Overhearing the conversation between David and Saul, Jonathan does not see the giant's head in David's hands; all he sees is his heart. Jonathan's spirit quickens and he knows in that moment he is called to help David fulfil his calling. In the middle, we have to know how to discern between two types of alignments that will approach our lives—those who are spirit-led and those who are self-seeking.

In the Goliath moments, you will find Sauls will come to control you, but Jonathans are sent to release you. Jonathan became a brother to David while Saul wanted to become David's manager. David had to discern which relationship he was going to give his allegiance and loyalty to. On my journey, I have found that Jonathans are some of the greatest relational miracles God hides in our middle moments. But you will never find them if you become overimpressed with Saul. You need to know the fame that Saul may offer can never compare to the vow that Jonathan wants to make with you.

COVENANT OR CONTROL

In 1 Samuel 18:2, Saul wanted to control David, but Jonathan wanted to make a covenant. Covenant relationships are based on something far greater than your successes or failures; they are centred in Christ and focused in faith. They want to position you for your future, not fasten you to your past. They want what God wants for your life, not what they want for theirs. Covenants are not selfish—they don't have an agenda to use you, but rather they are looking for ways to contribute to you.

Saul was not interested in a covenant. He wanted to control David's success. And he was not happy when David's popularity appeared to be greater than his own. Saul-type relationships will contain you in the middle. They will build a fence around your success and use your giant-killing skills to further their own purposes. They will make your unscheduled stop their tourist trap—selling Goliath memorabilia and making you known for the killing, rather than your calling. By all means, let Goliath moments refine you, but make sure that they don't define you! Don't accept the badge of "giant killer" when you are destined to wear the crown of a king; don't become known as the man who held a giant's head when you could be known as the man after God's own heart.

When we allow others to contain us in our challenge or our triumph, we reduce our capacity. A wrong alignment can derail our God-given assignment. Saul's insecurity would eventually attempt to sabotage David's journey. Saul went from befriending David to trying to assassinate him, as David's successes highlighted all the more Saul's failures.

Saul-friendships will always require you to produce more giant-head moments. When the supply runs out, then the friendship becomes strained. I have found that those who attach to my life for something I have, over who I am, soon leave my life for something else.

Be careful why people attach to you; understand the context and the conversations that you have in these moments. If people become your friend in the middle because they empathize with your sorrow, they may not be able to stay attached to you if you turn that sorrow into rejoicing. Some people want to make your misery their common bond. They want to feed the pain instead of lead you to the place of healing. They want to make your discomfort their gathering point. Maybe they see in you a common offense and they want to become your offense keeper. They will gladly help remind you of the offense and keep you up-to-date on the progress of your offender; they will follow them for you on Twitter and pass on any more information that will hold you for longer in the place you were supposed to have left long ago.

COVENANT RELATIONSHIPS ARE BASED ON SOMETHING FAR GREATER THAN YOUR SUCCESSES OR FAILURES.

If your tragedy will attract people to your journey, how much more will your success? Are the people who come to you there because of your gift in business, music, and ability to draw a crowd or entertain? Are they there for what you have or whom you know? They may want to use the attachment to attract their own piece of the action. David arrived on that battleground with no friends—even his own brothers had told him he was not welcome!

> When Eliab, David's oldest brother, heard him speaking with the men, he burned with anger at him and asked, "Why have you come down here? And with whom did you leave those few sheep in the wilderness? I know how conceited you are and how wicked your heart is; you came down only to watch the battle." (1 Samuel 17:28)

Where his own brothers dismissed David, God had a brother waiting who would embrace David wholeheartedly. This brother was not bound by blood but by spirit. Jonathan would become more of a brother to David than his own. He would love him in a way that was selfless and without any sting. Jonathan was the friend that saw his future and was determined to help him get there no matter the cost.

JONATHAN COMPANY

Jonathans are in every journey, but often we never find them because we are so disappointed by our own brother's response— the one we thought would be there, but then never showed up.

Unfortunately, these people tend to get more attention than the ones who are there for us and who are ready to do whatever it takes. Learn how to spot a Jonathan, and listen for his conversation. He speaks in a way that your spirit understands. Don't allow your flesh to dictate your friends, but allow God to guide you to those who have the same spirit.

We all need people in those pit-stop moments that have no other agenda than getting to the finish line. You don't want the person whose job it is to refuel your car hankering a secret ambition to drive your car. Jonathan-type friends are the ones who are secure to serve. They are fulfilled in playing their part and have no desire to be the whole. They are confident in what they bring, and they happily celebrate what you bring. They are sent by God to be on your side, to join your journey and enhance your adventure. They come with the tools you need to get the job done. They have skills and wisdom, but even better than that, they have the same spirit.

JONATHANS ARE A MIRACLE IN THE MIDDLE, AND WHEN YOU FIND THEM THEY WILL CAPTURE YOUR HEART.

Jonathan was only on David's team for a short period of time. But in that time, he made one of the greatest contributions: he protected David, defended and fought for him—even when that meant standing against his own father. Jonathans are a miracle in the middle, and when you find them they will capture your heart. You will feel like you have known them all your life. And when it comes time—as it sometimes does—for them to leave, you, like David, may weep as you will be forever grateful for their invaluable contribution to your journey. I have learned that even when Jonathans have to leave your journey, they never leave your life. They will always be part of the team; they are carried in your heart. They are a constant voice of encouragement in the background of your mind. You can hear them cheering you on, affirming your calling, and shouting to your spirit, "Keep going!" In fact, one of the greatest miracles I have discovered in the middle are the Jonathans God has hidden there waiting for me.

ACTION POINTS

1. Remove the things from your life that are holding you back from your destiny.
2. Refuse to make a temporary stopping point your permanent dwelling.
3. Do not allow your giant moments to define you.

PRAYER POINTS

1. Pray that you would see people over procession.
2. Pray for Jonathan company on your journey.
3. Pray and give thanks for the covenant relationships in your life.

ELEVEN

MIRACLE IN THE MIDDLE

IF I TOLD YOU I WAS CURRENTLY IN THE FRONT PASSENGER seat of a car being driven from a conference in Munich to another conference in Zurich—while my Swiss-German speaking hosts are attempting to drive as smoothly as possible so I can type these words as efficiently as possible—would you believe me? Well, probably by this point in the book, you would. All of our journeys are filled with less than ideal, challenging, and sometimes, just strange circumstances. So here I am, in the middle of being driven from one place to the next, writing the words of what has become the final chapter you are now reading. I'm in between the two destinations that are expecting me to speak, writing words I was not expecting to write, so that they can speak to you. We all live in those middle moments.

Middle moments aren't meant to be tolerated; they are to be points of acceleration. And they don't have to be wasted. With the right approach, they can become an opportunity for you to discover things you never even knew were within you.

When we find meaning in our middle, we help give meaning to another's. That's why I want to encourage you to keep your eyes open! While in the middle, don't allow the circumstances, the pressure, or even the boredom to cause you to fall asleep to the potential that is all around you and within you.

DEADLINES

The truth is, sometimes we need the right motivation to change our attitude in the middle. At times, we need encouragement. Sometimes we need to find more strength and support. But often, we actually need something a little less popular, but extremely effective—we need a deadline. The reason I flipped my laptop open and started typing with a precariously balanced keyboard on my knee and coffee in my hand, was not because I felt a sudden surge of inspiration by the scenery around me, moving me to write. If the truth were known, I would rather be curled up on the backseat of the car with my shades on, enjoying a few hours of sleep. The only reason I'm writing during this car journey is because of a deadline. I had a date when the manuscript was expected to be sent to my patient publishing team, and that deadline was set, whether I liked it or not. The deadline was at the forefront of my mind, and therefore, it motivated me in my middle to be active and not passive.

I have a love-hate relationship with deadlines; I don't like the demands they make, but I do appreciate the results they yield. Deadlines are those expectations calling to be fulfilled; they are the vow that needs to be honored and the commitment that needs you to show up. As much as I may complain about them, without them my life and yours would read very differently.

When the disciples got in the boat that day in Mark 6, and pushed away from the shore, they had a deadline—a place they were expected to arrive called Bethsaida. Bethsaida was their deadline destination. They didn't have weeks to make the journey, they had hours. There was no time for visiting other shores; the place had been decided and the deadline set. Jesus was going to be meeting them in Bethsaida, and He was the kind of date you did not want to stand up. And yet there are times when, if we are honest, we have done just that—we have not shown up where we were supposed to, when we were supposed to. When God said go, we stayed. When He said change, we remained the same. We stood up a date with our future because we weren't ready to put the work into the required journey. In the middle, our spiritual timekeeping is tested as we must decide what dominates us more—our present problem or our future promise.

DEADLINES ARE A POWERFUL TOOL IN THE MIDDLE.

Deadlines are a calling card to your future and are often the thing that adds just enough pressure to make you persevere when you have the opportunity to quit. If you set no deadline on your hurts, you will never move to the place of healing. If you put no deadline on your bitterness, you will never get better. If you have no deadline on your insecurity, then you will never move to feeling secure.

When our daughter started high school a whole new level of expectations came with the new level of education. Now she has daily homework assignments given by her various teachers throughout the week, and each piece of homework comes with its own deadline. As a parent, I have learned that my job is to be the deadline monitor. When she first began to receive homework, she would pay little attention to the pending deadline. The result was many last-minute frenzies of activity, as the realization the homework she had not given any attention to over the last few days was now all due on the same day. As a result, panic would take over and the homework meltdown would begin. After this happened several times, we knew it was time to change our homework routine. We needed to make deadlines our friend rather than our enemy; they needed to be something we worked toward rather than ignored. Paying attention to the deadline made the homework achievable. It meant we could make a plan of action so that tasks didn't clash, and it wasn't all being done at the same time. The deadlines actually began to make the homework more bearable and, dare I say, even more enjoyable.

Soon, our daughter came to understand that the teacher was not trying to punish her with these deadlines, but was trying to help her progress more quickly through her course work. The failure to meet them would not make the homework disappear; it would simply make the work go on for longer than it should. The same is true for our own journey through life. We can either learn the lessons faster or revisit them later. But I have discovered ignoring the deadlines does not make the lesson disappear; it just delays the lesson being learned.

When Jesus recruited the twelve, they were on a tight deadline. Over the next three years, He was going to teach them many lessons and send them a lot of homework. He knew when

His time came to go to the cross class was going to be dismissed. They were going to move from students to teachers, from fishermen to fishers of men, and He wanted to set them up to succeed. So Jesus put them on a fast-track learning course. He would teach them how to keep moving forward, how to not get stuck in places where the message was not well received, how to shake the dust off their feet and keep going. He would also teach them how to deal with the crowds efficiently and order the masses accordingly.

KEEP THE FAITH

Jesus helped the disciples bring order to the chaos and clarity into the confusion. Jesus even told them when He was going to the cross and that there would be a three-day deadline for His return. He told them this so that in the middle they would not freak out, go backward, lose perspective, or despair. But even with the deadline for the resurrection set, some disciples still could not wait for it to be fulfilled. Instead of staying where Jesus said He would meet them, they headed away from Jerusalem and down the road to Emmaus.

> Now that same day two of them were going to a village called Emmaus, about seven miles from Jerusalem. They were talking with each other about everything that had happened. As they talked and discussed these things with each other, Jesus himself came up and walked along with them; but they were kept from recognizing him. (Luke 24:13–16)

The disciples struggled to keep their faith in the middle—confused and scared for their future, many left Jesus. Others were grieving and doubting they would ever see Him again. Though He had made his three-day schedule clear, not everyone had their eyes open watching and waiting for His word to be fulfilled. Even when Jesus walked next to the disciples on the road to Emmaus, they still didn't realize it was Him until after He had left them and moved on. So, too, when we take our eyes off our deadline we can miss the point, forget the purpose for our persistence, and quit prematurely.

As we come to the close of this book, I want to encourage you in your current middle to assign yourself some homework and place some deadlines on things that have gone on for too long. How would your current experience change if you were to set some deadlines? What about setting an end date for that unforgiveness or on your procrastination? How about a deadline to ask that person that question, make that deal? I honestly believe some deadlines could make some people a lot happier a lot faster than they thought possible.

TIME'S UP

In 2 Samuel, we read of King David's adulterous relationship with Uriah's wife, and how she conceived and gave birth to a baby. In chapter 12, we read about how the baby was struck ill as a consequence of David's sin.

Nathan replied, "The LORD has taken away your sin. You are not going to die. But because by doing this you have shown

utter contempt for the LORD, the son born to you will die."
(vv. 13–14)

While the baby was ill, David faced a terrible middle—one of grief and regret, sorrow and repentance. As he lay for seven days in a place of solitude and sorrow, he waited to see what would happen. David was waiting for God's judgment. He had set himself a deadline. When God responded, so would David. He determined that whatever the outcome he would accept God's judgment and move forward. On the seventh day, David heard his servants whispering and asked about his child. They let him know of the infant's death. At this news, David's behavior changed.

> "Is the child dead?" he asked. "Yes," they replied, "he is dead."
> Then David got up from the ground. After he had washed, put on lotions and changed his clothes, he went into the house of the LORD and worshiped. Then he went to his own house, and at his request they served him food, and he ate. (vv. 19–20)

David's response shocked some around him. Why did he go wash himself and change his clothes at that time? Why would he not grieve longer now that the child had died? David had set himself a grieving deadline. He gave his grief an expiration date. God's answer would be the point at which he would change his behavior. He would accept what he could not change, and change what he could—which was his own attitude and actions. Whether David felt like it or not, he was going to go worship. He was going to get up, go be with his wife, and he was going to resume his duties. Deadlines are a powerful tool in the middle. If we use them wisely we can move forward in spite of our feelings.

EXPIRATION DATE

You would not eat food after its expiration date—the date that tells you what was once good for you and full of nutrients has now become spoiled and rotten. This date protects you from putting something inside your body that will make you sick. An expiration date does not mean you can't eat the food, it just means that you need to eat it within a certain time frame. How about applying that principle to your life? What if when the offense comes, you give it an expiration date. You work out what needs to be worked out in your own heart, but then when it's time, like David, you get up, get washed, worship, and change your clothes. What about giving that relationship that was once good for you, but has now become toxic, an expiration date? It is not helping you grow anymore, and the more you put the toxic conversations into your spirit, the worse you will feel. It's time to get up and move on. Don't wait for God to give you all the deadlines. When you know something is close to its expiration date, deal with it. Psalm 30:5 says,

> For his anger lasts only a moment, but his favor lasts a life-
> time; weeping may stay for the night, but rejoicing comes in
> the morning.

Even God has made His anger only last for a moment; He has placed a deadline on it and His grace and mercy are renewed every morning. You don't have to trade on yesterday's mercy when He has a fresh supply every day!

FINAL CALL

Imagine for a moment that the things God has planned for your life—the opportunities, the connections He wants you to make, the things He wants you to pursue and possess—were like the flight departure times for a trip you were scheduled to take. After selecting the destination, you book the ticket. Now it's your responsibility to keep to the schedule and turn up at the right place at the right time.

The plane has a set flight time and it is going to leave for the agreed destination with or without you. Every passenger that's scheduled to make the trip is entrusted with the same information—the times they need to check in and board the plane. Sometimes, we treat our relationship with God like it is a private plane arrangement.

WE ARE NOT CALLED TO FLY SOLO AND SET OUR OWN ITINERARIES.

We want to go where we want, when we want, and we don't care about the other passengers, as we will get there in our own time. On the contrary, I have found with God it's less of the private plane scenario and more often scheduled flights.

All of our lives are connected to a much bigger picture, and all of our paths are destined at set junctures to interconnect with others. We are not called to fly solo and set our own itineraries. We are called to connect and travel with the others God has scheduled for the same destination. Therefore, we have to pay more attention to the call of God and be where He wants us to be when He wants us to be there. Just like the PA system in the airport announcing the boarding of a particular flight, you have to hear the call and make sure you show up before they close the gate.

I find myself constantly reminding my son that planes don't wait for people, but people need to be on time for their planes. As much as we travel, you would think our kids would understand this. For the most part they do, but every now and then, Noah, in particular, can't see why the pilot won't change his flight time to allow the cartoon he is engrossed in at the airport lounge to finish—or why he can't wait while Noah stops and has a burger.

When Noah was younger, no matter what we said, he would not believe any pilot would leave him behind. He couldn't imagine an airplane he had a ticket for would take off without him. In his mind, Noah thought the pilot's plans would revolve around his. He couldn't understand that the pilot was concerned with a much bigger picture, like all of the other passengers, the places that were expecting him, and the small window of time he had to make his departure safely. To Noah, this was all irrelevant information. Too often, in our immature and self-centred ways of thinking, we can view our journey from the same vantage point. We can become so preoccupied with our agenda that we fail to understand God's bigger picture. We fail to see the necessity of the other passengers we are supposed to travel with, or the connecting flights we are destined to make. One day, however, Noah was taught a lesson he would never forget, and ever since that day, we have never been late for a flight.

WAKE UP

We were heading from Phoenix to California and our destination was Disneyland. It was one of the most exciting days any six-year-old could have on their calendar. The only problem for our six-year-old was that we had chosen a flight that was leaving extremely early. As every parent who has ever been to Disneyland will understand, when you pay that much to see a mouse you are going to get every minute your Disney dollars have paid for. So the very earliest flight we could find to get us into the park before lunchtime was what we booked. That early flight meant an even earlier wake-up call. But that morning, nobody was moving fast, even after several failed attempts to get the kids out of bed—including both myself and my husband jumping on their beds with them still under the covers singing a loud rendition of "It's a Small World After All."

Eventually, we got every sleepy, and slightly cranky, soul into the car. Then we hit the traffic. Frustrated by the slow-moving vehicles, the stress mounted and the happiest place on earth seemed a million miles away. We dashed to drop off our rental car, and then ran into the airport to check in for our flight, only to find the longest line I had ever seen at a Southwest check-in counter. When we arrived at the counter with the baggage drop, we were told that due to our late arrival for check-in, they could not get us onto the flight. We had missed the plane to Disneyland!

In that moment, my six-year-old learned a hard reality: a pilot could and would leave without you. He realized it was not an empty threat his parents had used to avoid stopping for a burger or sweets, but it was actually true! The plane could take off without him! In that moment, Noah's jaw dropped and his tears started to fall as he clutched his Mickey Mouse in horror. "You mean they are leaving without us?" As I answered "yes," Noah's world fell apart. Then his sister began to blame Noah for her missed flight too. The feeling of missing the very thing you had been saving for and waiting for, all because you couldn't get out of bed fast enough, was not a good feeling. But sometimes, it's the only way we will learn that if God gives us a plane time, we'd better make sure we check in early.

Fortunately, for all concerned, the lady behind the desk began searching for another way to help our family upon seeing the emotional meltdown I was managing. Both kids started praying with passion for an answer. Within a few moments she turned into the kids' superhero as she announced, "I have another flight." We were all rescheduled to fly to Disneyland a few hours later. After kissing the flight attendant, we checked in and went early to our gate to sit and wait for the next flight. And the kids moved from traumatized to deliriously happy.

That's a window into how God's grace works when we miss our deadlines. He doesn't leave us stranded at the airport; He reschedules our flights. His grace will issue us a new ticket for a different time. Just remember that the flight you missed could have gotten you to where you desired to be sooner. It was our inability to mobilize more quickly that morning that cost us more time living the dream at Disney.

I want to encourage you to look again at God's Word and the things He has spoken into your heart. Let Him bring to mind some of the gate calls that He has for your life. Tune your ear to the nudge that's telling you it's time to go and board that flight. Whatever He is asking you to take care of, determine to see it through. If He's told you to sow the money, do it; if He said to go and take the job, then go get it; if He told you to speak up, then find your voice. Don't keep the plane waiting and don't miss your destination.

Ten spies held up an entire generation from catching their flight. They reported the land God had already given them was too hard to possess. Though God had set a destination and put out the gate call, they were denied entry because of the delay the bad report created. That bad report affected not just the ten, but tens of thousands of people, who would never get to the land that flowed with milk and honey. They would trade God's dream destination for desert living.

Be careful of the voices you listen to. Travel with those who are more determined to get you there than they are in keeping you comfortable. Make friends who keep their deadlines—those who don't always wait for the very last call to board, because hanging around in that company makes for very stressful living. And if you find yourself reading this right now, then guess what, you have a deadline to thank. Though I did not like it at the time, I appreciated its results. It made me reach a finishing line, it gave me the joy of completion, and it got this book out of my heart and into your hands.

LAND AHOY!

Sometimes God will give us a clear picture of where we are going, but many other times, He will just point us in the right direction—allowing the next shore to become clearer with every stroke we take. In the middle, the disciples could not yet

see what was waiting for them, but they knew if they kept rowing it would soon become clearer. What if you knew by taking
three more strokes with that oar, you would be able to see the
land your seasick heart longs for? What it you knew that in a
few more days you would be done with this season and the next
one would begin? Sometimes, even when we don't see, we have
to row as if we have.

It was said of those heroes of the faith who went before us in
Hebrews 11:13:

> All these people were still living by faith when they died.
> They did not receive the things promised; they only saw them
> and welcomed them from a distance.

That's the behavior I want in my middle. To wave to my
future from afar, to row like I am about to bump into the next
shore, to push those oars through the water with purpose,
believing the land is near.

We must constantly remember that God is on our side. He
wants us to make it! He is planning great things for us. God is
a good God and has plans to do good for you, for me, and
through us. He plans to prosper us and not to harm us
(Jeremiah 29:11), and promises to provide paddle power. It should spur us on to keep rowing
since we know God is waiting in our future with great things
planned.

WE MUST CONSTANTLY REMEMBER THAT GOD IS ON OUR SIDE.

Sometimes in the middle we need to put verses like this
on repeat. We need to hear the good reports and take all the

encouragement we can from those who have sailed similar seas—like the heroes of the faith who left us a legacy of hope to hold onto. We need to become those same voices when others face a void. We need to shout to each other's vessels to keep rowing, you are closer than you think. We need to look out for one another and inform the other vessels in the middle that there is land ahoy. We need those who have found the shore called restoration to shout land ahoy to those who are rowing through brokenness. We need those who have been through loss to shout out there's land ahoy called peace! We need those who have faced sickness to shout, "Keep rowing to your healing."

JUST KEEP ROWING

One of my favorite scenes in the movie *Finding Nemo* is at the very end. After Nemo has been reunited with his father and they are heading home, they are faced with yet another disaster. When all of the fish are caught up in a trawler's net, all of a sudden Nemo—realizing they are about to die in that net—begins to take charge. Even though his father is fearful and tries to hold him back, the little fish is determined to help the other fish live. So he devises a plan. The plan is that everybody has to swim down. So they just keep swimming down and as they do, they begin to chant, "Keep swimming, just keep swimming, keep swimming, just keep swimming." Chanting and swimming, they eventually break the net and all the fish are freed.

When I watched that again recently, I was struck by the power that small capture held. What if we were to do the same? What if in the middle we got a chant going to "Just keep rowing, just keep rowing"? What if we all decided to help each other break through our middles so we could embrace the more God has for us? How many people could we save? How many nets could be broken? As a pastor, I want our church to chant "keep rowing" to one another. As a wife, I want to encourage my husband with "just keep rowing." As a mom, when my kids want to quit, I want to whisper, "Just keep rowing." When my friends want to settle for less than God's best, I want to nudge them to keep rowing. And as an author, I want to write books that say to you, my friend, "Keep rowing, just keep rowing. You are closer to your freedom than you think."

JESUS REVEALED

Have you ever thought you knew someone really well and then they did something that completely caught you off guard? Awhile back, we had several friends over for dinner. Among our dinner guests were our good pals Ben and Debbie, who we have known for some time. They lead a charity called Hope for Justice, rescuing victims of human trafficking. They are incredible leaders and freedom fighters, and also a lot of fun. So that night, when we were

THE MIDDLE INTRODUCED THEM TO THE WATER- **WALKING JESUS.**

all enjoying the conversation at our dining room table, we weren't expecting to discover that our friend Ben was also a secret opera star. I am not sure what led to the big reveal moment, but at some point in the evening, as several of us were chatting and laughing, Ben pushed his chair away from the table and delivered the most beautiful piece of Italian opera. As he came to his big finish, we all sat stunned. Several had tearstained faces, moved by this amazing piece of music he had just performed.

That night over dinner, a new side to our friend was revealed. From that point on, not only did we see Ben as a freedom fighter, but we also saw Ben as an opera singer. When I asked him why he hadn't revealed this hidden talent before, he answered, "Because there had never been an occasion that called for it."

When he said that, I was reminded of how it can be on our journey with God. We don't see every facet of His power or wisdom up front. We simply could not handle it. When Moses was about to see God, he was only able to see a glimpse of His back, and that was almost too much for him to take. Our relationship with Jesus is one that unfolds along the journey, and the more you journey with Him, the more of Him you discover. And it's often in those middle moments that more of who Jesus is will be revealed.

They say you should save the best for last. I am not sure if that's always true, but on this occasion I have saved my favorite part of the Mark 6 story we have been studying for the last section of this book. After the disciples had strained at the oars for a while, it says Jesus came to them on the water.

> He saw the disciples straining at the oars, because the wind
> was against them. Shortly before dawn he went out to them,
> walking on the lake. (v. 48)

Did you just catch that Jesus showed up in a way that they had never seen before? They had been with Jesus in many different situations—they had seen Him heal, teach, take authority over demons, and challenge religious legalism. They had seen His compassion to the littlest children and His temper that turned over the money lenders' tables. They knew Jesus more than most, but the middle was about to reveal to them a Jesus they had never seen before. The middle introduced them to the water-walking Jesus.

Everybody on the shores had seen the Jesus with sand under His sandals. The crowds had touched the Jesus that walked amongst them on the streets, and they had sat and seen the Jesus who taught them on the hillsides. But this Jesus the crowds didn't see. This Jesus couldn't be touched. This Jesus, even the disciples failed to recognize—actually thinking they were seeing a ghost. This Jesus had the power to make the waves His walkway and to silence the storm. From this point forward, the Jesus they discovered in the middle would change their understanding of who He was.

The revealed Jesus was a miracle in the middle! Jesus will reveal Himself to you as a miracle in your middle, too, because it's in those middle moments that you see His power like you've never seen it on the shores. It's in those moments you see that His grace has no end and that His mercy has new depths. In the middle He will become Abba Father. He will be your Miracle Provider. In the middle He is your Water-Walking Miracle.

There have been moments in my journey where I have felt so weary, lost, hurt, and confused. But when I have looked up from the mess, I've felt God's presence in a way that I've never felt it before. I have called to Jesus in a way I never knew I could call on His Name. In the middle I have learned how to let Jesus hold me in a way that my time on the shore never showed me. On the shores you sing songs about Jesus being your friend. But in the middle you experience how much of a friend He truly is. On the shores you can say He is your all in all, but in the storm He becomes all you have. In my middle moments I have seen how His love runs so much deeper, how His grace is such unmerited favor, and how His forgiveness is without measure. In the middle times when I have battled sickness, I have moved from knowing He can heal to seeing Jesus heal me. I have gone from saying God is able to Him being revealed as my more-than-enough. The greatest miracle in the middle is the Jesus that it reveals to me.

Jesus has so many facets and aspects to Him; He has so many ways to be love, to show love; He has layer upon layer for the ways He provides, cares, and guides our life. Our understanding of His greatness is so small, our ability to comprehend His power is so limited, and that's why we must never stop looking for the Jesus that our middle will reveal.

MY PRAYER

As I close this book, my prayer for you, my friend, is that you would see just how far you have already come and just how much more God has for you on the next shore. I pray that you would take your eyes off the wind and waves and look for the water-walking Jesus who is your miracle in the middle.

I pray that you would pick back up the oars on your marriage, business, family, and calling. I am shouting to you to just keep rowing, just keep rowing. I want to remind you that there are things waiting for you on the shores of Bethsaida, where God told you to go. He wants you to arrive at your destination—with the seed your storm has given you ready to be sown into the lives of others—to strengthen their struggle and to give purpose to their pain. So when your life bumps up on your next shore, be ready to share your story. Reveal your Jesus and magnify the miracles that can only be found in the middle.

ACTION POINTS

1. Where do you need to set some deadlines?
2. How can you encourage others to keep rowing?
3. Write down the miracle that you are believing to see in your middle.

PRAYER POINTS

1. Pray for ways that you can be an encourager to others in their middle.
2. Pray for ways that you can share the Jesus who has been revealed to you.
3. Thank God in advance for your miracle in the middle.

ABOUT THE AUTHOR

CHARLOTTE GAMBILL HAS AN INFECTIOUS LOVE FOR LIFE, A deep love for people, and a zealous love for God's House. Her passion is to build the local church across the earth, to see people reach their full potential, and to develop and strengthen leadership. Charlotte is known for her practical, humorous, and passionate application of God's Word. Her messages of life and purpose are rallying a generation to embrace the broken and become ambassadors of hope. Charlotte is also a speaker and leads Life Church in England with her husband, Steve, and together they have two children, Hope Cherish and Noah Brave.